Awakening to the Animal

Kingdom

by Robert Shapiro and Julie Rapkin

Cassandra Press
San Rafael, Ca. 94915

Cassandra Press
P.O. Box 868
San Rafael, Ca. 94915

Printed in the United States of America.

First printing 1989

ISBN 0-945946-02-3

Library of Congress Catalogue Card Number 88-63543

Front cover art and illustrations by Susan St. Thomas. Copyright © 1989 Cassandra Press.

Table of Contents

Editors Note

I feel that it is essential to mention that all of the ideas presented in this book do not necessarily represent or agree with the beliefs of the editor. In support of the channeler himself, I chose to include specific controversial material that otherwise may not have been printed. I found the editing of this book to be a growth process which required a willingness to "agree to disagree." It amazed me to discover that risk taking was a necessary ingredient in publishing the thoughts of these animals and that channeling is a process that requires the loosening of controls.

I want to share with you two humorously synchronistic events that occurred while I was typing the passages for the dog and whale sections of this book. In the middle of working with the dog material, two dogs that I have never seen in my neighborhood came joyfully bounding to the back door of my house. I felt strongly that they were expressing their encouragement and approval of the project I was undertaking, and they practically insisted on coming inside to my work area. A few hours after that experience, I began working on the whale material. A voice from the back bedroom shouted "Turn on the television," because a special on whales was just beginning. Again, I felt this to be a validation from these wonderful creatures that we call animals, that we are all very much connected in body, mind, and spirit.

Julie Rapkin

Preface

In our exposure to the many different animal kingdoms that you will find in this book, one theme is echoed over and over. That is the idea that each species is willing to be a very specific aspect of behavior, a type of Beingness or a lifestyle that many of us can identify with. The theme is repeated, "We look like this. We act like this. We represent some portion of the human potential and act as mirror reflections to all human beings." This is no accident, but clearly has been an answer to our need to be surrounded with symbolic stimulations and situations for growth.

In this day and age, we are called to recognize the "oneness" of all life. Indeed, we are stimulated constantly toward the idea that the Earth itself, as a planet, is a living being. Publications such as *The Global Brain* by Peter Russel, for example, make a clear and vital case for this concept. In the age of specialization that many of us have grown up in, we have been overexposed to (and expected to live up to) the finite rather then the infinite. This has led us toward a life of separation, encapsulation, and egocentric thinking. Now we clearly see that, in this our atomic age, cooperation, mutual understanding, and harmony are no longer luxuries of the philosopher. Indeed, such problems as pollution of air, water, and land, seemingly incurable diseases, and high rates of unemployment, do not honor the boundaries of nations or states.

All of the planetary beings now have the challenge of integration, not just as a people but in the individual sense as well. This integration must be simple and practical so that we will apply it in our day-to-day reality.

If we can be offered and can accept the guidance of those who live a naturally balanced and uncomplicated life (the animals), perhaps we will see our own simplicity and turn our complex life onto an easier path. The guidance in this book is designed to ease your way onto this path.

Introduction

I am speaking to you as the Great Guardian Spirit of all animals as well as of mankind. I would like those of you who read this book to consider several points. Your world has not been living up to it's potential in recent years. You have had the opportunity to see how your world looks from space so that you could see the beauty of it's natural color and harmony. When you look back upon the Earth, you may see it is a whole and complete entity unto itself. The purpose of this vision is to remind you of your own wholeness, and that you are all a portion of some greater Oneness. If you did not agree with the opinion of one of your toes, would you simply shoot it off and dispose of it nearby? Certainly not! When you discard a species of animal, you do the same. You discard a portion of yourself. As mankind, your task is to be curious and full of wonder, as an explorer race. Your task in completion, is to remain curious as an equal to all species that live upon this planet. There is no disconnection between you and all other species.

The purpose of this book is not to criticize you or to say that you are wrong or bad. It is to remind you that you are of the One and that your purpose in being of the One is to allow you to assimilate all of the growth available here on this planet. You can come to an understanding of yourself in wholeness and completeness. I encourage you to explore the animal species with this outlook.

In future issues, we may discuss the plant kingdom, the mineral kingdom, and other portions of mankind's world here on Earth.

For now, your mission is to simply understand how you fit integrally within the animal kingdom. It is not an accident that there are similarities between you and many species of the animal kingdom. The similarities go beyond the biological or microbiological levels. It is my intention to remind you of your harmonious existence with all that lives around you, so that you may come to a greater understanding of your total self, the Earth.

When you read portions of this book about animals, notice how they do not lecture you. They understand their integral harmony with all of the Earth and recognize their portion of the whole. Please see how you fit into the entire scheme. Notice how many of the aspects that an animal stands for reflect aspects of your own consciousness. This is done to reveal to you your own purpose for being here on the Earth, and that, my friends, is simply to become more of yourselves in comfort. Read this book with enjoyment and curiosity, and begin to explore your world as an equal with dominion rather then as a dominant force.

Chapter I

Bears

We are the bears and our representation to you as a race is the combined values of grace and strength. We represent the combined values of femininity and masculinity. It is our purpose to show you how it is possible to have joyful ways and strength simultaneously. Your race has misinterpreted the bears as a species of ferocious beasts. Those who have hunted us know better then anyone else that our real personality is playful. We are climbers to the tops of tall trees. We are creatures that enjoy making a game out of obtaining sustenance. When we seek food, we will make a fun experience out of it, such as fishing. Your species has seen us as ferocious, as in the idea of the Grizzly Bear. Most of us now are strictly fun loving.

We originated in the star system that you refer to as Sirius, which is a system that has done much experimenting with potential races of beings. We were created on Sirius through the use of emotional stimulation, of grace and strength. Your race stands for curiosity, wonderment, and exploration. In the same sense, we have at our basis emotions that are stimulated and created into matter. There are matter form creation machines that excite energy, plasmic energy, through a form of high frequency stimulation of dense matter. The frequency stimulation is using a form of emotions. The beings who are the creators will stimulate the machine with these emotions, running through what you would call crystal energizing devices, to focus the emotions into a confined space. This will then, in conjunction with the plasmic energy within that space, create a being which definitively expresses these emotions. There will be a range of potentials shown. Our species was among this range of potentials, and was deemed best by those who seeded us here on this planet. Our species can easily adapt to the extremes of weather that you have shown on this planet. We come from a small planet in the Sirius star group where experimental life is created.

We have existed in a form on Saturn, although there is no vast quantity of life on the surface. There is some life just below the surface. We exist in a form there that is different from the form that exists here on this planet. It is much smaller and has a shell rather then fur, in order to tolerate the radiation that penetrates the inside of the planet. We also exist at a higher frequency, in a less dense and not exactly physical form, on an outpost of the planet Pluto. Once a

civilization is established within a planet there is not the problem of the surface rages that may occur. We have a few representatives there.

The human beings use the name bear for us. We have a race name that is closer reflected by the word Hybernia. We do not understand the human language as words, but instead our primary mode of communication is a form of telepathic communion. We use guttural/vocal sounds to indicate more immediate needs. That's a survival language. When you are involved in your lower chakra survival energy, you may yell to each other and may not necessarily use words. Our main communication, however, is telepathic. We pass on our racial heritage, the messages of our origin, and where we will go when we cease to exist, in a telepathic mode.

When we die, we return in our soul forms to a unit soul. That is a mass soul, or mass-consciousness soul, which has a strong tie to our planet of origin. It also has a strong tie to this planet. We return, in some ways, to a dimension of consciousness that is not physical. We circle into that dimension for a short period of time in order to reassess whether or not we will re-image ourselves on your planet. Depending upon where we are needed, we may reincarnate into the past, present, or the future.

We recognize that your species has hunted us for food and clothing, as well as for cultural needs. Some tribal cultures have needed to experience our energies though eating, wearing of our fur coats, or through experiencing our energies in order to increase their own strength. The tribal hunters have hunted us, and once their blood is enriched by our blood through the consumption of our flesh, or even through a familiarity with our bodies, there is a physical/emotional experience of who we are. It is important for you to recognize that we may choose to reincarnate at a time when we are needed by a tribal culture as a source of food or as a source of warmth. Western culture mainly uses us as a sample species for study.

We understand the need for man to hunt and to consume our bodies, since we do this as well. We will assume the identities of that which we eat. As we hunt and make a game of hunting other species, we take upon ourselves their abilities to survive. When we hunt in the water for fish, we are able to survive because of the adaptation to the fish environment which is enhanced by our eating their flesh.

If you do choose to hunt us, we would appreciate it if you would include an expression of honor. It is not often that a member of our species will allow itself to be captured by human beings these days. There are dwindling numbers of us in this influenced Earth because there is less need for us at this time. Your twentieth century civilization is so spread out upon the planet that the need for us has dwindled. I will ask that if you do hunt for us, guard against the killing of the old wise ones. The wise ones, the older bears, are frequently the ones that look after larger herds of us. We would also appreciate it if when we are consumed in the hunting method, it be in a mode that includes honor.

Should you take one of us and bring us back to your civilization for consumption or for wearing the fur, we would appreciate it if you would leave some gift in the forest. Leave some portion of yourself, just as we will leave some portion of ourselves wherever we go through natural acts of elimination. Even though you may feel that it is a strange request, I will ask you to eliminate or evacuate your waste products and leave some portion of yourself in the forest. In this way, the forest will know physically that you have been there.

I will also ask that you do not use high-powered rifles. I would request that the bow and arrow, even the more mechanized forms, be used more frequently. Our species provides energy to groups that are more tribal; the bow and arrow is a more primitive weapon. For those of you using rifles, we feel that there is less of a connection and appreciation. You can stand in the distance and fire upon us. As a result, you may never make a personal connection with who we are in our lives. This personal connection is very important.

In many tribal cultures, there is a ceremony or dance performed before they go out to seek one of us. In this act, they will in effect call to us, as a species, and ask one or two of us to come forward to enrich their souls though the consumption of our bodies. We understand this very well. Usually, one or two of us will volunteer, or come forth to be consumed by the tribe in this way. Our bodies will not only add to their physical comfort, but will strengthen them as a race. This is a portion of life here on this Earth. Those of you who choose to continue to hunt with rifles, we ask that you do some form of ritual that will call out to us. We ask that, before you go hunting, you draw a picture. It does not have to be a work of art, just a picture that represents to you a bear that you would like to bring home. This way, a message will be received by us. Please draw this picture and touch it with your hands; imagine being out in the woods with us. Whether a member of our species will come home with you depends upon your need as perceived by our race. However, it will put into the ethers a telepathic communion of your message and your need. Put your emotional, physical, mental, and spiritual energy into your connection with this drawing. That might allow you to form a connection with a member of our species that it is proper for you to connect with. Please make it more personal. It will not just be going out to hunt for the sake of hunting as a sport.

Hunting is rarely done to support and supplement the human race and its need to understand itself through identification with its own planet. Understand that my constant referral to the tribal races is because the tribal races will frequently understand the gift that is offered; they will use every last portion of our physical bodies so that we do not feel that we are simply being shot and carried home as a trophy. Recognize that we understand your need and desire to conquer all powerful species so that you feel that you are in control of your lives. We will ask you not to hunt us with the idea of simply hanging us on a wall some place. It is much more appropriate if we are consumed by you. We strongly urge any and all hunters to be involved with us in some ritualistic way before the hunt. We will ask you to at least wear the fur, or touch the fur, or to eat some small portion of the meat so that you will be strengthened. We ask this because it is important for you to recognize who we are. You, as a carnivorous species, must realize this through a physical act.

It is less necessary for us to exist in this time period, and that is why we are considered an endangered species. The mechanization of your western world does not really include our true enriching value within your culture as something necessary to your survival. Even though we may seem to disappear, we will continue to reincarnate in the past and future according to need. Even if an animal species seems to disappear completely from existence on the planet, it is always likely that there will be within the genetic structure of the Earth the memory of that being. The physical matter that was once a portion of our body will seed the planet and can be used as a genetic calling card to draw our spirits toward the Earth. We may incarnate on a place where we have once lived. This is why I referred to the elimination and the leaving of products that have been evacuated from the body. This material includes within it the genetic code of that which has eliminated it. This can then be utilized in a form of matter, turned to soil, and used by some other creature. The genetic code material as well as the flesh of the being becomes a portion of the Earth.

We dream in a waking state, when our survival instinct is not needed to protect us. We are able to connect with our mass-consciousness identity of Hybernia though others of our species, especially the older ones. They have had all the knowledge of Hybernia passed on to them. We are in a state of wakefulness and maintain a meditative state, camouflage ourselves, and supplement our knowledge of Hybernia with information that is most applicable to our current geographic location. It is a form of daydreaming. When we sleep we join our race consciousness in the soul state. When we hibernate we also rejoin the Hybernia consciousness to reassess whether we will continue to live another physical year on this planet, or whether we allow our bodies to be taken and consumed by some other form of life. We will spend a considerable amount of time in a state that is very similar to suspended animation, in which we will live much more consciously in our spirit life. It is also during hibernation time that medicine people of various tribes can more easily experience our bodies on the soul level and can experience the energy of who we are.

Our act of procreation is symbolic in the sense that it is a physical attunement or invitation of one of our species to pass through, just as it is with your human race. We have a ritual that we do in which we send out ultrasonic sounds. It is possible for you to record these sounds in the wild, although it is extremely unlikely that you will hear this when we are in captivity. Your attitude toward us when we are in captivity is not one of true communion, but rather one of scientific observation. In the wild, we allow our ultrasonic sound to attract just the right member of our species who chooses to reincarnate through us physically.

The lesson that the bear has to teach mankind is the ability to walk with power and yet walk gently on the land. It has been noted, by those who have observed and studied us, that there is a playful side to our nature even though we can become protective. We walk in a very graceful fashion. Your western culture has chosen to think of us as being large and lumbering. Those who have hunted us in our natural element know that we are powerful as well as graceful physically. Man can receive, through the bear, the gift of walking lightly on the Earth with strength and safety.

Chapter II

Cats

The age of cats began when man was first getting in touch with his ideas of separation. Cats were created by man as an idea relating to the individual sexes, almost a transitional medium between the sexes to unite them. Cats balance the energies of male and female. Cats have the innate power to lend each sex aspects of the other. It is why we have been greatly loved or deeply distrusted.

Cats in your lives represent a unique awareness of Self, an intense awakening of your union with spirit. Cats are very aware of your actions. A cat will sometimes raise one eye and you will notice a sudden appeal to the wit, the charm, the silliness of the cat. They can be anything that you want them to be, but they will always react directly to your personality and your energy.

You will find that what you are thinking is not the only energy a cat will react to. Many times cats will not do what is expected of them. What is expected of them is created from the conscious mind. Rather they may do things that are unexpected and whimsical and not always popular (knocking over the cookie jar and sitting in it). They will react to what is going on within you on an emotional level. They are reacting to your subtle bodies, that portion of you of which you are not consciously aware, but which sends out "needs" just the same. They will show you who you are, at any moment. You may notice the next time you are with or around cats, that if you are thinking too much, they may loose their interest in you. On the other hand, if you are involved in intense emotional feelings, you will undoubtedly get their attention.

Purring is designed in cats to create a sense of calm in human beings. You may notice that very rarely do cats sit off by themselves, without human beings in close proximity, and purr. Cats purr for you, because it calms you. Is it possible for a cat to be curled up in your lap purring, and for you not to be calmed and warmed by it? You may be thinking, "This cat really likes me," or "I sure have a way with animals."

Cats are in your lives to support you; nonetheless, we will not cooperate with joy when you choose to spay or neuter us. We are in your lives and are adapted to live with mankind. We know why we are here. We were designed to be a reflection and to fit your needs. Forms of larger wild cats have their own way of maintaining population control through the natural food chain, providing nourishment for others and returning to the land. The domestic cat is not a natural form. We cannot take birth control pills as does man. We have private pet status and are no longer connected to the wild. You must either allow the cat population to be consumed by other animals without deciding it is wrong, or you must continue to go on altering us. I'm not telling you to include a coyote in your household. I am saying that it is not healthy for us if you are afraid to let us go outside. Please let us out so that we can touch the Earth with our feet. If you don't let us out we may become strange.

The best way to encourage our growth is to allow us to be natural. This doesn't mean allowing us to make little deposits on your expensive new carpet, but it does mean letting us go outside. If the neighborhood dog chases us, don't throw rocks at the dog, because this is part of the game right now. The dogs chase us, and we chase the birds; it's part of a natural cycle. Nurture us by letting us go outdoors, and go outdoors yourself. As you connect to the Earth and embrace her, you will then realize what is natural for her and for us. Notice how nature lives in harmony. As you become more aware of the harmony, consciously and emotionally, you will find that cats will be more nurtured as well. We will feel your sense of harmony with the Earth and that will feed us.

Sometimes a cat will hunt a beautiful bird, chew it up in front of you, deposit it at your doorstep and seem to say proudly, "Here, a gift for you." The cat is letting you know what life is really about for animals. Death is in continuity. That bird has put its life into me voluntarily. That bird allowed itself to join its brother cat's body, and return to the Earth through the cat. Cats will always feel themselves connected to the One Great Spirit. This is why the cycle of consumption in the food chain does not bring about an end to our existence. We become another existence. We are fully connected with the Great Spirit and are involved with it at all times. Any single cat can tie you into any other cat you have ever known. All you need to do is to imagine having a conversation with a cat and allow yourself to hear the answer. Within any one cat there is a total cat spirit.

In our presence, a genuine condition of change can take place. People feel differently when we are about, especially if they are not receiving certain attributes which would help them to be more in balance. We are providers of what mankind needs to receive; we create a field of energy that affects the subtle body of mankind. A black space or a hole may occur in the subtle body, or auric field of an individual. An aspect of what you ascribe to be masculine or feminine traits is always involved with these holes. When we are in your presence, we stimulate these areas and coordinate the wave length energy that is beamed around these holes. We balance and set up a neutral field energy within these holes; we cannot alter your experience, but we can smooth it over. If you are willing to receive it, we can stimulate your energy field, and set up a more receptive state for you.

If you do develop one of these holes within your energy field, it is only a form of response to one of your needs. If you feel unworthy, for example, you may create a form of disease or discomfort. Then, you will cease to emanate and receive the light at a particular portion of your physical body. It is as though you turned off the light in that area.

When we are present, we do several things. We cannot cure you, but we can, by emanating balancing energy, create a condition wherein that negative field energy is neutralized. We cannot change your experience to a positive one, but we can balance your experience into a state in which you are more receptive to your own healing process. We assist you in balancing your energies, but we do not create the healing. Only you can create that, in your infinite wisdom. As individuals and as task masters of your own experience, you have created a belief system that requires you to have certain experiences. Some of these experiences are positive and loving, others are less joyous. You have a choice to grow and to come into the greater knowledge that you possess, when you are interacting in a greater way with your light body. At other times, you are so involved in your physical body that you want to believe that your physical world (as you have created it) in fact creates you.

When you believe that you are separate from the world that you experience, you may feel that you require outside assistance. We, as cats, reflect back to you portions of your experience. As cats we act as channels of amplification of your own creative energy to assist you physically, as well as to stimulate you mentally and emotionally into connection with your Spiritual, All Knowingness. As explained before, the physical assistance in energy balancing for you is stimulated through your creation of us in your lives. The actual process involves our connection with your subtle body or your Light Self, and creation of a spiritual readiness to allow the body to heal itself. In that sense, we are a link (that you have created) to stimulate this healing condition within your Total Self. We do not heal you in anyway; we are not outside of your existence. You create us in your lives as intermediaries for your subtle body, to fill the gap that you have created in your own auric or light field. As you create a negative gap, you create us in your lives to maintain a neutral energy balance and to stimulate you into receiving a positive energy balance.

The auric field is made up of both positive and negative energy fields and is in balance with your experienced world. You may become more dense and attract to that portion of your physical body a heaviness which acts as a form of an energy drain, or hole. You create for yourself a need for balance which we will fill.

Other animals assist with this also, but we are more well known for this. Horses, camels, llamas and animals of this family provide a similar service. Dogs do not provide this service but instead provide joy and warmth, among other wonderful characteristics.

You may ask, "Why have we created cats, and what is the myth and mystery of cats in our experienced world?" Our creation precedes the ancient days of Egypt. There was an elite priest class (which interacted with a high form of intelligence) that created the idea of a telekinetic balancing tool to act as an energy amplifier. The reference to telekinesis here does not mean that we transport ourselves around in a state of invisibility. It does mean that we can, working through your own creative ability, transport or juggle energies within your own subtle body to interact telekinetically with your experienced world. We replace the lapses in your auric field with energy experienced from another life form.

You are a creature that experiences a linear life span, or one life after another as if time were flowing as a river from and towards enlightenment. You will never, in that river of evolving lives, create the identical discomfort zone within any of your physical bodies. Thus, we act as a bridge between your separate but constant lives (past, present, and future) as a conductor. When you are experiencing a hole in your auric field, we can interact with your other lives and utilize energy that you created in those lives, thereby acting as a bridge to stimulate that exact portion of your auric field. You have created us in your lives as a form of priest class tool, almost like an animal magic wand. Magic has always been ascribed to the high priest class, those who have knowledge outside that of the general population. The word magic had evolved to describe that which is understood only by a select few.

We were created long ago by one of these priest classes to be a tool which functions to connect you (in your light body awareness) with all of your lives. Within each and every one of your lives you grow and have slightly separate lessons that you learn. We act as a tool, almost like a computer, to select that life which would have the most beneficial experience for you at the spiritual body level and bring into you the energy from that portion of your life energy structure.

It was understood in Atlantean times that there was a need to control man's emotional field. Emotions were understood to be a powerful force, used to adjust man's inner experience with his outer experienced world. A high priest class, in the place that you refer to as Atlantis, experimented with creatures and incorporated certain genetic structures into their emotional and subtle fields. They used our own harmonic pituitary and adrenal glands within our physical bodies. Upon examining these glands within the cat body, you would not find much physical similarity between the cat and human bodies, but you would find the energy harmonics in these glands to be very similar. This harmonic connection works like a radio frequency to establish constant contact between us and human beings through the emotional body. This constant form of frequency contact, reveals this compatibility that emanates through the glandular structures. We were created by this priest class to act as a link for them to amplify their own energy fields in these areas. They were beginning from a condition of being in balance. However, it was their desire to accentuate their own energy fields in these areas to create a greater understanding for themselves of how they could engineer social interactions between human beings. We, as experimental creatures, were a tool of design which seemed to have a life of it's own.

Today, many people have more then one cat and sometimes many, many cats. There is a subtle knowingness within each and every one of you that there is something about us that creates in you a need for "more." You will many times confuse this need for "more" with a need for more cats in your lives. The true need is for more contact with human beings. In your mental society, it is through contact with other human beings that you discover your lessons and the purpose for life on this planet. The need for "more" that you may feel when cats are around is a need for more human contact or stimulation of your own greater knowledge. We were created to stimulate the priest class to greater understanding of what society requires to create a more attuned state of interaction between beings. A belief was set up by them that required outside stimulation of their own awareness. They did not really need this, but they believed they needed stimulation.

In the Atlantean society, crystals were used to a great extent to amplify energy fields. One thought of the time was that a higher amplification device was needed from outside the experienced consciousness. Why was that priest class not satisfied with the use of crystals? This class traveled to other societies that were less technologically advanced, where the use of crystals would have been thought to be only magic and not accepted. If they felt that the priest class was using tools that were outside of their experienced world, they would not trust them and would become less cooperative. These priests utilized the genetic sciences of the time (which were highly evolved technologically) and created this disguised amplification device that you now call cats.

Their word for us at that time was Ki-tones; this is an actual sound from their language, not a translation into your language. If you took that word apart and spelled it in your language, key-tones, the direct translation would mean harmonics. In that sense, we were used as were all crystals, in the tonal harmonic structure to stimulate and balance energies and form a greater compatibility with any experience. We "key-tones" were utilized to help the priest class social engineers move freely through other cultures. It was easy for them to move through cultures utilizing us as harmonic instruments. They were not in a position to influence those other cultures directly. You might say that we were spy tools. They could have forced their way upon these other societies using crystals, but they understood that in order to have a greater compatibility a creature who would be of curious and stimulating interest would be more useful. We allowed a greater accessibility to these cultures outside of the Atlantean society. The word was abbreviated to Keyt and then Kat or Cat.

Any greater understanding of an idea or interaction with another culture does not require a form of outside amplification. It only requires a greater connection to your own light body Self. As all creatures do, we show you what you are experiencing in your total consciousness by our actions. If we become ill when we are living with you, that illness represents something in your life that requires study. It is our way of saying, "Look now at that portion of your physical body and what it represents to you, that we show to you in our bodies as discomfort. Look now, look quickly, before you create discomfort for yourself in this symbolic area." We will interact with your own discomfort, or lack of worthiness, to show you the area of need in any one of your lives.

Your subtle or light body is that portion of your energy which creates experiences for you at the physical level. You create your physical forms so that you may interact with other physical forms. This helps to remind you of your position in the total world that you experience. You can continue in your experienced world to utilize cats in the stimulation of your own experience. I suggest that you no longer become enamored with us to the extreme of having fifty of us in your experienced individual life. Please become more aware of the lessons that we can teach you. A cat in your life can help you to balance your own energy field and bring you into a greater understanding of yourself as functioning between all of your past, present, and future lives. We will not do the work for you, but if you utilize a form of meditation, we can still function to sharpen your perceptive abilities of other cultures.

Consider lying down in some calm, peaceful environment where you will not be disturbed. If you have a cat in the room, so much the better, but you can also use your imagination to picture us in your mind.

Pretend to be in a cat body. Imagine walking around the room or wherever you are; explore the room with your paws, your sense of touch, smell, taste, and in other ways you may have seen us interact with our surroundings.

The purpose of this exercise is to help you to understand your own ability to experience the sub-tleties that make up life and to exercise your emotions through a link-up to your brain's power of imagination. In this way, you can also make better contact with us as a species.

In time, as you practice this exercise, see if you can pick out one of our species that you particularly like (perhaps one of us living with you, although that is not a requirement). Pretend to be in the body of that cat and see what you feel. It may be fun!

Through the years, we have been altered by you (at the subtle body level) so that we no longer function to assist you to alter the creations interculturally, as we did in Atlantean times. You have found other ways to influence various cultures without utilizing tools such as cats. War is really a way of forcing your own cultural needs onto another culture. The idea of control originated from a need to dominate the conditions of one's experienced world, from outside a knowledge of Self-creation.

Each and every one of you create your exterior world, and you need not perpetuate the idea of one race of people being better then another. You don't have to have another serving you in order to make you greater then you already are. If one society sets up its goals and aims as being more right or more justifiable than that of another society, this will lead toward domination. Domination is a belief that grows out of control. You now have the choice for domination or dominion. Dominion grows out of contact with your Spiritual Self. Remember that, as you create the idea that you must control your external world from outside of yourself, so you will believe that your physical world is all there is. There is a greater idea that works with you to guide you. We cats remind you that you can act within a larger idea of yourself. You can be in greater connection with your idea of God/Goddess/All That Is if you are willing to interact with your fellow beings in a more loving way and do not force your beliefs on others. You are all a portion of the greater One. You can truly influence your own lives in harmony, instead of through the idea of control.

Chapter III

Cattle

I am here, near you now, standing on all fours (as you would say). There is Earth under my hoofs. I am surrounded by my fellows. We recognize the distinct smell of each other. This is good. I am comforted by the knowledge that I am with my fellow beings. There are sounds of machinery nearby and voices of men who are working. There are also occasional stares and eye contact between us and those outside the pen. Sometimes there are moments of romance or sentiment, a touching feeling. Then there is the breaking of eye contact. We would like to encourage you to be friendly towards us and to appreciate all that we have to offer.

I represent those beings you call cattle or beef. We are here for you, in your life. Do not feel that you are at war with us and hail your conquering victory by eating our flesh. This is not so. We have no war with you whatsoever, even though you raise us and nurture our flesh and then consume that flesh. For in fact, we live on the Earth. We look at the Earth in each other. Our connection is totally to the Earth. We are creatures of it and are blessed by it. In your own way, you have chosen to reach into the Earth, to consume the Earth, through us. We do not consume each other. We, as a group of beings, consume only that which is grown on the Earth. We understand that your consumption of us is a continuation of those events that perpetuate and bind you, not as a prisoner, but as a loved one, to the soil upon which you are now standing. It is important that you understand that your relationship to the Earth is more then what you eat and how you eat it, and who becomes part of you. Our communications are more or less physical. We have a herd instinct. As a group, we tend to move in the same direction though occasionally one of us will wander off by himself. We communicate through sounds and touch. We do not understand the human languages. We respond to being touched and do what someone wants us to do. Human beings herd us because it is necessary for a form of touching to take place there. If the herd is all one sex, there is no dominance except that which is provided by the human being. The dominant bull in a mixed herd has a degree of authority over those whom he has physical contact with.

We have strong sexual drives, and feel the need to carry on our species. We procreate much more often then you may encourage us to. It is very common for mankind to choose to mate us in specific pairs. If we are on our own, which is very rare, then we will choose our own mates.

We do not dream with layered experiences. We go into a relaxed meditative state. When you hear us lowing, we are in a semi-somnambulant dream state. In our deep sleep state, we achieve relaxation and are involved with our original herd as well as connected with those that were present at our birth (this may include human beings). Lowing condition requires peace and calm and usually takes place away from mankind.

We have a form of physical alteration that happens within our body that allows us to adapt to extreme winter temperatures. We have layers of fat that can build up, if we are well fed, that will help our heat distribution. For some of the more wild of our species, we will create a physical/molecular change within our bodies to survive harsher winter conditions without suffering any serious problems. We must, however, have enough food and the ability to move around freely. If the snow gets too deep, we sometimes have problems.

Should you be consuming a hot-dog or a hamburger, do not feel that you are somehow denying my right to live. Do not be convinced that you are in any way less holy than those who do not eat of the flesh. It is true that those who do not eat flesh will have less consciousness dependency upon the Earth in order to live. They will be able and willing and desirous of expanding their consciousness beyond the Earth plane. However, the Earth plane is valid and glorious and fun. For those of you who do eat our flesh you will find that your Earth life can be more fun, more physical. The lusty pleasures of our Earth can be experienced in greater magnitude. Your contact with the Earth can be more amplified by our inclusion in your lives.

Now, does that mean that you have to eat our flesh? Not necessarily. You may wear our skin on your shoes. Another way is to have us live amongst you, to allow us to be and not consume us, to allow us to be where we choose. I know that that is not always convenient. But if we were not raised and multiplied artificially, our numbers would reduce to no more than three to five thousand over the entire Earth (due to such forces as other animals that prey upon us and eat our flesh). I do not condemn you for eating us and using our bodies, but I do caution you not to overlook the possibilities of allowing yourself to be in contact with us without consuming us.

In some countries a form of creature much like us, the ox, is revered, not just for the labor it performs, but for its Being as well. In certain countries, it is believed that the ox possesses the attractive force to receive the souls of mankind, to harbor and enrich those souls, and to allow them to perpetuate a continuum. They remain in contact with the Earth even though those souls no longer occupy a physical human body. In India, as it is called, this creature is not consumed as you would consume us. People live with the creature, with this Being. I am not suggesting that you do this in your country, in this United States. What I am suggesting is that you try (those of you who do not eat meat) to see if you can locate or seek one of us out, but not for the purpose of feeling sorry for us. We are here because mankind has manifested us for the purpose of exposing itself to us, of experiencing us.

If we choose to allow it, you may touch one of us. If that is not comfortable, then just look at us and pretend to be inside of us. Not so that you would know fear, for we do not know fear until the exact moment of death. Rather, do this to experience our reception of Earth. For those of you who eat only plants, understand that plants reach for the Sun as they grow. Even sea plants reach for the light.

We cattle or beef see the Earth. We do not stare at the sky. We appreciate the light, we enjoy the light. We stare at the Earth. We look at the Earth, not with rejection, not with dejection, but with humble gratification for receiving our gifts. We have the understanding of the power and of what is created here. We see that a society can live in mutual nurturing and harmony. Balance can be maintained through the cooperation of all life forms, including our own. Do not your so-called vegetarians condemn your fellow meat-eating mankind? In truth, they only seek to live in peace, harmony, and tranquility and to enjoy the pleasures of Earth. Understand, those of you who do not eat meat, that if you cannot bring us into your bodies physically, you must find another way to bring us and other creatures like us into your body. Imagine you are inside us, to experience our joy of living on the surface of the planet.

Some of you will get out of balance in reaching toward higher forms of consciousness and you will lose touch with the harmony of the Earth. To stay in touch with that harmony, it is important for you to acquire a new awareness and belief and understanding. Know that you can have balance and enjoy the pleasures of Earth as well as the pleasures of what you call higher consciousness at the same time. That will require your bringing into yourself a balance, a joy of living on planet Earth, an embracing of planet Earth and of your higher consciousness. In this way, planet Earth will be your home. It will also be your place of salvation and nurturing in tolerance and in love.

The question is asked, "How do we feel about people who work in slaughterhouses, or killing houses?" Understand that we realize our manifestation on your planet is brought about by mankind's perceived need to consume our flesh to maintain his comfortable style of living, as well as to use our skin and other portions of our bodies to maintain that comfort. Understand that we know this, it is not a surprise. We do not resent those who physically destroy our bodies. This does not mean, however, that we enjoy being destroyed or that we forgive liberties taken in the destruction of our bodies.

We understand that in an occupation that creates a science or a mechanization out of killing, in order to preserve one's sanity and love of self, it is almost necessary at times to incorporate a form of madness. This includes what you might call a bizarre sense of humor in order to maintain one's sense of self worth. I refer to jokes that are performed with our bodies, after our destruction and sometimes be fore. We do not approve of this or take it lightly. We do understand that it is done out of a need to compensate for feelings of negative self worth. All children are raised in your religions with a sanctity toward life. Those who choose to work in these places, these killing grounds, are persuaded to do so out of a need to preserve their own families and themselves. Yet, in order to do this they must often go against the morals taught to them as children and even young adults. This type of challenge to their sensibilities is sometimes more then they can stand. They will joke, or scream, or carry on in ways that might be unseemly to the world outside of such a place. They will do this to preserve their sanity. For this is not pretty work, it is not happy work, it is not fun. Yet mankind's search for peace, joy, tranquility, and harmony must be served. Even in a negative situation, mankind will seek to create some form of joy, even though it may be bizarre or discomforting to other beings. It is with this knowledge that I answer this question.

We do not hate those workers. We do not resent them. We do not consider them to be our enemies. We consider them to be servers of mankind's needs, just as we are. We will play out our roles for as long as you require it. We do ask any readers who work in these killing places to please treat us with respect.

Understand that it is natural for us to be nervous. When you go to destroy our bodies, treat us with respect; in this way, your respect will be comforting. You will feel more important and more worthwhile in your community. Do not be ashamed of what you do. The work you do is not pleasant and is frequently looked upon with disdain by your fellow mankind, but remember that your work is important to those who eat our flesh, and wear our skin. See how you fit into the system that has been created. Understand that we are all of the greater All. No act done to one by one, goes ignored by the All, just as no act done by one for one, is ignored by the All. All is known, and all is felt, and all is remembered. Seek to balance the scale of injustice you have created for yourself. Look not for enemies who have forced you to work in such a place; rather, look upon your fellow man and his needs and realize that you are serving, just as you are served by others.

Long ago, mankind brought forth from his consciousness a need to create a connection with himself and the planet. Mankind could not fly, it was beyond his physical expression, so he experienced the birds. Mankind could not swim for hours underwater, so he choose to experience the fishes. Mankind could not believe that he had any part in creating creatures who walk, swim, and fly on the Earth. He chose to believe in a God apart from himself. Just remember that mankind chose to create, that mankind is the God you seek outside of yourselves. Mankind/womankind is the absolute epitome of the final expression and the ultimate Beingness on Earth. Remember that Earth is a God entity unto itself. The higher expression beyond Earth is merely another way of living. God exists as the All, and Earth is of the All, and mankind, creatures, plants, rocks, stones, and trees are of the All. We are God and all God-consciousness. Please remember this so that you do not deny yourself your own creative power of beauty and harmony. If you should feel that God is apart from you, you will never understand that God is a portion of you to be recognized and experienced.

You are evolving in your consciousness toward becoming more than you have allowed yourself to be. It is important to understand your connection to

Earth and why you are here. You are here merely to discover that your light or soul selves exist in the presence of all light, of all knowledge at all times, no matter where you are.

Chapter IV

Deers and Does

We of the doe consciousness represent the feminine principle in mankind. This does not mean only that portion of the principle which aligns itself with women, it also means that which aligns itself with men. For in truth, all beings—mankind, womankind, or creature—have the masculine and feminine principles within them. We help to represent that in our own way.

We originally derived from the species unicorn, which has been considered to be a mythical animal. The unicorn is not really a horse-like creature as is sometimes pictured. It is the size of fully grown deer, but is also similar to a horse. It has the muscular structure of a horse and the bodily shape of a deer. The traditional horn in the center of it's forehead, is not straight, but is slightly curved. There have been no fossilized remains of the unicorn found on this planet because the species was moved to a distant planet when its survival was threatened by outside forces. They were resettled in very small numbers. The unicorn species was not quite fully adapted to the Earth in it's current dimension, and we were perceived to be a more hearty species that had a better chance of survival. We were created here by a highly technological civilization that once existed on this planet.

We always know when we are going to die. This is frequently stimulated by a feeling of malaise or gradual discomfort that occurs within our bodies. We are not by nature uncomfortable. If we start feeling tired, or we have been severely injured, or we know that it is time to pass over into another species as food, we understand the meaning. Our soul consciousness, our essence, will return to the center of the Earth (where our originators still exist to some extent). We will, in time, be returned to where we are needed.

Many times, one of us allows itself to be killed by an automobile because it knows that it is time to move on. This is not a suicide, but is a voluntary termination. If you do not choose to participate in that experience, you might attach some object to your car to create a slight sound, not a sound that would not disturb you, but one that would alter our perception of your automobile. If some kind of low-key sound is emitted by the vehicle, other than the motor noise, which sometimes blends into the background of the wind, we will know that you are coming and perhaps not choose *you* as a participant in our termination. Understand that there are no accidental deaths.

We do not need to understand the human language, because we understand the human instinct. We are in touch with the human chakra system, the first, second and some of the third chakra. It is unnecessary for us to be in touch with the human fourth chakra because it has not developed sufficiently to communicate with us consciously. We will communicate with the human beings' survival instinct. We can tell what you are going to do before you do it, by the energy that you are in at that moment. The very best hunters can kill us because they are able to stop thinking while they are involved in the hunt. They stop thinking, and they concentrate on something other then their own body consciousness.

We communicate to each other primarily telepathically and will not make a great deal of sound. Sounds are rather uncommon for us. We do have the facility to make sounds, which will most often be a kind of hissing sound (an air release sound). We usually communicate telepathically and instantaneously.

We have a form of dream that allows us to leap great distances between planets (traveling by the soul line, or astral traveling). We will sometimes go to where the unicorns live (since they are our ancestors) and encourage them to tell us stories about how it used to be and how it will be on the Earth in the future. We have a pleasant experience in our dream state.

We experience time and space as bookends. We have times when we are drawn to each other to procreate, and it is during these times that we will feel the need to have open-hearted love. We are very much a loving species so we will be drawn toward each other by a magnetic flux that we each have. We tend to stay in the family unit.

It is our job to represent the nurturing, the softness, the receptive qualities that mankind truly needs to develop. In truth, the female of your species has for sometime been the receptive one, while the males have been the projective or powerful ones, like the buck in our species. In our species, the bucks not only represent that which projects, they represent the heart and soul, as well as strength and courage.

Know that mankind's ability to move forward is not hampered in any way by his sense of limitation or restriction. It is only your belief in limitation and restriction that slows you down. Sometimes it is necessary to receive and be nurtured by others in order to build up your strength again and influence your world for the greater good.

You will find that there are times that you will simply lack the understanding to know what is right for yourself. At those moments, it is good to be able to receive nurturing from your friends and from those who may not even know you personally. These people will be able to help you if you can reach a hand toward them. Not a hand that stops them from helping you, but a hand that requests the assistance. Understand that you need to learn how to receive as well as to give.

Mankind's consciousness has been predicated in large part upon giving. In some cases this is charity as you perceive it, sharing with others. In other cases, this charity has gone out of bounds, beyond the motivation that started it. When you reach into another culture or group of people to give your knowledge to them, make certain that they ask for it first. For indeed, different human cultures have their own special gifts to share with each other, and perhaps with you as well. Do not always assume that your way is the best way. Perhaps it is the only way you know, but that does not make it the best way or the only way. It is merely the way you know. Always be open to the ideas and ideals of others. For indeed it is possible that you might learn something to make your life better, rather than something that will confuse you or make your life more complicated. Always be aware that life is for the tasting and sampling. Be always ready to receive our message in the form of this loving nurturing. Your fellow beings are awaiting you around every corner, on every block, just off in the next field, over the next hill, in the next town. Your fellow beings await you, to share with you their way of life. Do not believe that any one way is the only way.

You are all unique, all of you Beings. You have your own unique contributions to offer the world. However, you must learn how to receive the uniqueness of others, without trying to force your uniqueness on them. Always know that you can accomplish anything that you set out to do, but many times you will have to ask for help from your fellows. Know that your life is in the making every moment, and in order to allow it be the very best life, you have only to allow your fellow beings to assist you. In this way you can best receive guidance from all your fellows, brothers and sisters, and children as well. Many times, in your own words, "Out of the mouths of babes," does great wisdom come. Do not always seek the complicated solutions, even if the questions are complicated. Many times, the simplest solutions offer the simplest cures. Indeed, your own recognition of each other as being unique and very special Beings is enough as a beginning.

Do not then thrust yourself on others, forcing your type of consciousness or life on them. Wait first, and see what they have to say, what they have to offer you. In truth, this may be your own unique and most valuable contribution to yourself. If you can accept what is being offered by others without being threatened, without feeling that you must change in order to come into the comfort zone and the reality structure of other people, if you can just hear and see if they have a special ingredient, you can add a great deal to your own life. It is the finest gift you can give yourself. You might say it is sampling the smorgasbord of life. Indeed, if you travel all over the world, you will never find two beings, in mankind or in the animal kingdom, that are exactly alike. You will, however, find many who are similar. There will always be those who are so unique that they stand out as being representatives of a new species, and you are not certain what species that may be. These are the finest, as they represent the qualities that mankind searches for so frequently. They have that ability to say, "I am unique." Be aware my friends, it is useful and good to state to yourself and to the world, "I am unique." Don't let anyone tell you that you are just like anyone else. No one is just like anyone else. You are all unique. Be able to receive from your fellows. In this way you can truly give the very finest you have to offer. It will be colored with many rainbows from your fellow beings.

Chapter V

Dinosaurs

You may notice that in your past cultures, as well as your present culture, there is a sense of affection bordering on an almost extreme attraction by the human race for dinosaurs. You might guess that human beings would be afraid of the damage we could have done, according to how you picture our size and bulk. Mankind represents our race as both a malevolent and benevolent species. Malevolent represented by our portrayal as monsters in the movies and benevolent by our representation as cartoons and playthings for children. The attraction to the dinosaur kingdom is one that is very deep in your roots. Dinosaurs are not living among you now physically, but we serve as reminders of what once was. Since there seems to be an enormous popularity to the idea of dinosaurs, we have chosen to be included in this book.

Our species, while it seems to predate yours by millions or billions of years, is from a time on your planet when there was no clearcut understanding of whether this would be a place for animals or human beings. Since there was a decision, by the Creator, to allow this planet to have the higher life forms in all of its varied races, it was necessary to displace or eliminate some of the creatures that would find living with the human being awkward. If anything, including an animal species, has ever existed on this planet, it continues in space and time. Largely, we have returned to the mass consciousness where our wisdom and experience can be called upon by those who need us.

Your scientists may agree that your solar system is made up of material from one single origin, and therefore it is not unusual that there is wildlife which would have traits that are adaptable to several of the planets. We originated in the galaxy known as Sirius and we still have some remnants or remains there, as well as on Earth. We are studied on Sirius by races that have a cellular structure not unlike our own. We communicate largely through emotional transmission, an almost ultrasonic and emotional encouragement. We do not exactly communicate through speech, though we may make noises if we have the ability to do so. The communication utilizes a sound wave system in which we make ourselves known to each other. The awareness of our culture and the perpetuation of our intelligence, such as you are reading now, is something that is extended from the universal mass consciousness.

When we were in an embodied state, and if there was no danger present, we would become aware in our sleep states of certain colors. If danger was present while we were sleeping, we would see a shade of red and wake up prepared. We believe it was possible that we did dream of some things, but they might have been conditions rather then specific events. Sometimes, we would have images that would pop into our head where we would see almost human being type creatures who would have a form of reptilian presence about them, and we would feel that they were some type of distant cousin.

The historical aspect of the darker side of mankind's nature, is easily symbolized by what we represent. Dinosaurs, by our very size, attest to the "beastly" side of life. Due to mankind's evolution in integrating his desires for living a higher form of life on a daily basis, that is to say, manifesting your ideas and your goals as your day to day reality, the darker side of mankind is currently coming to the fore to be represented. Mankind's change to this higher form of consciousness, will allow him to move past war, greed, and selfishness. The avoidance of confrontation and integration with the darker side of your nature is preventing your race from unifying on this planet. As you come into a time of reforming your own consciousness into an image that is one that goes beyond your more "animalistic" motivations, you will be confronted (psychologically speaking) with the primitive elements of your personality. The consciousness of the dinosaur is upon you so that you can all move beyond the darker elements of your old ways and begin to change them. You have changed from malevolence to benevolence in the way you have judged us. Our darker side has been permitted to change into something benign.

The savage aspect of your nature is actually part of your physical make up. The challenge is to become aware that children can choose to represent the "beast" and can experience the terror and dominance that is possible. This type of life can be quick, fast, and furious. It may seem like an adventure, but it will be over all too soon. Or they may choose the more benign and childlike approach, and may appear to be surrounded by "wild animals" as their peers. They can develop strength and challenge those who are involved in savageness to reach a higher level through acceptance of themselves, instead of hatred. We salute the children of this planet for this tremendously difficult task they have taken upon themselves. We suggest to the adults that you do not assume that childhood is what it was for you. In order for childhood to be that magical experience that you would like to think it is, you will have to pay attention to the "real" world and do what you can to improve it.

Now is a time when mankind throughout all of his philosophies, not only the so-called New Age enlightenment, but also the higher aspirations of religion and philosophical practice, is striving towards a peaceful co-existence out of necessity. As a result, it is as though you are on an agenda which is not completely clear to you. Somewhere a hidden chime has gone off within most of your heads to say, "Now you must begin to work seriously towards world peace." Many of you have the ability to be not only self-destructive but to destroy the future life potential on this planet. We are not simply referring to atomic and chemical weapons or other forms of well-known and understood annihilation systems, but rather the more insidious threat of pollution and ecological imbalance.

We understand that fossil fuel can be used for other purposes then for burning, and we hope that in time it will be used in other ways. There are certain portions of it, that have the ability, if refined properly, to assist the Earth in coming back to an ecological balance. These are organic enzymes that when combined with the residual organic components of petroleum (as it exists as a fluid) and when added to areas of polluted organic based materials (sludge), will change it into something more benign. It is likely that science will discover this catalytic action and produce these "pollution eaters" within the next five to ten years, due to the need. It is ironic that fossil fuel is available in large quantities and that it appears that this fluid is contributing rather extensively to the pollution problem. The field of pollution science is undoubtedly the job of the future.

Through years of scientific exploration and simply recognizing that people get along better under certain circumstances, usually crisis-oriented, there has become a form of almost hidden sub-plot to mankind's destiny. It is known by many people that if there is an extreme crisis or threat, the damn breaks and everyone must rush to higher ground, that people will rally around each other. Those who may not even like each other under normal circumstances will rush to each other's aid. In other words, emergency situations call for emergency changes within social systems. As a result, it has been believed by your subconscious reality, that is to say, the subconscious mind of each and every one of you, that the best possible way to unite and come together peacefully, is through some form of crisis. For years you have considered the idea of making war that crisis. Now it is clear to cooler heads among your political hierarchies that war these days, with the weapons that you have, could be terminal for everyone.

There has been this hidden subconscious desire for a crisis in which everyone could rally around and it appears that the choice has been made to use the planet's ecological imbalance for this. In the coming years, many of the things that you have taken for granted will become almost luxurious. Clean water and clean pure air will become commodities that will be bought, sold, and traded. It will be necessary, in order to work towards rebalancing the ecological systems on this planet, for there to be absolute and total world cooperation. There will be a need for greater understanding and educational programs beginning with the children, to understand how their bodies, families, and society can see this world in a universal family concept.

Mankind is beginning to recognize the wholeness of life through the pursuit of the sciences as well as an understanding of their interactions with each other. Medical doctors are clear in that they know that if some portion of the body is not functioning correctly and develops an infection, that infection can spread to the rest of the body and impair the working of the entire body. Mankind may soon understand that he is also a cell in the body of Earth.

Chapter VI

Dogs

The meaning of dogs in the life of man is to help mankind understand the idea of absolute devotion. Absolute unwavering devotion goes hand in hand with subjugation. Dogs that exist in the wild live for the pure free spirit of being wild dogs. The domesticated animals that you refer to as your pets are those who are speaking to you now.

We as dogs have originated on this planet, and we like it here. We have been around a long time and we can get along in the wild if we have to, but we choose to be in your life to remind you of the Earth. This is why we react strongly to creatures that owe their home base identity to other planets, and we may bark. When we see you coming home, we will often run at you and bark with joy and evoke that emotion within yourself. Every time we bark we breath the Mother Earth nourishment into our bodies. We are cycling the Earth energy through us all of the time. We use our mouths to explore the world, and that is why we chew so much. We were developed here on Earth as a hybridization of a species that was natural to Earth. You will sometimes find references to wild dogs. We are a variation of wild dogs. We are really an evolution of the Earth cycle. Earth is something that you have to dig your toes into. The Earth supports you by providing you with the food you eat and the air you breath.

If you introduce a new dog into an environment that already has a pet, you will want to avoid those dogs that have been bred for aggressiveness. If animals are raised together as puppies and kittens, they have a much greater chance of harmonizing. If animals meet for the first time as adults, it is unlikely that they will do anything other then form an uneasy truce.

It is really the dog's job to guard against that which comes from the outside. Dogs will represent their owners on the emotional and physical level. If a dog is aggressive and has a tendency to be a fighting dog, look toward the owner. Dogs and owners very often look alike, and this is no accident. Many dogs, if they don't look like you physically, will fit your temperament. Do not bring animals into your life to bring yourself in. Share animals in your life to bring yourself out. People who feel good about themselves will naturally attract animals, and often the animals will want to follow them home. Dogs are in your life to reflect your life, so you can do something about it.

When a pet dog dies, it returns to the pet angelic realm. We do not live there, even though some of you consider us to be angels. We will pass through that realm into the dog spirit Oneness, which is directly and totally connected to the Earth. At that point, we will choose where to reincarnate. It is unlikely for a dog soul to choose not to reincarnate.

For those surviving families that are left behind, just think about us in your fond memories, and don't give up on the dog world. Think about us and remember us in energy. It is very possible to attract us in a reincarnated form. If the family wants to take another dog in, wait about three months. Concentrate on our energy, and allow a portion of our soul to be attracted into another dog body. We may not reincarnate as the same species. When you go to the pet store or the pound, be in tune with the energy that you felt from us when we lived with you before. Recollect us, but don't be tied to our exact appearance or personality. See if you are drawn to another one in the species. On certain occasions, we will choose to reincarnate within a living dog. Some living dogs that have had difficult lives and are on death row at the animal shelter (animal prison) can join souls with the incoming spirit. We would then attempt to give you some kind of a signal or a message that we are in your presence. We will usually do something on an energy level that you will gravitate toward. Or we may gesture in a way that you would recognize from our life in our other body.

Always use your feelings with us because we are primarily involved in the emotional field of Earth. We understand emotion and sound, and we do not need to understand any other language. We communicate primarily through touch. If we must stand off at a distance, we will emanate emotion as a field energy. We will then communicate in something like a radio signal. It is an energy cycle of tone and feeling. If you say something very nice to us but use a harsh tone, we will respond to the tone and not the word. If you wish to communicate with us, just imagine that you are having a conversation with us. As children you used your imagination until you were told by adults to stop fantasizing. You were told that you were not allowed to have conversations with imaginative people. How many of you had imaginary playmates? Your mother or father may have come in and said, "Don't talk to thin air, people will think you are crazy! I don't see anyone, so obviously no one is there!" When you want to talk to your dog, past or present, allow yourself to regain use of your imagination by speaking to us and listening (with your imagination) for an answer. You can say something in your mind, or out loud to your present dog, and you will notice that it will turn around and make eye contact with you. It wants you to know that it is hearing you

Mankind has decided that dogs have specific roles in terms of domestic pets and that wild dogs are something else. If we were allowed to reproduce the same way that people reproduce, we would like that much better then being altered. Very often in the city life, there are too many of us born; instead of taking us to dog death row, it would be nice to take us out into the country. Some of us would return to living in the wild. Many of you are threatened by the idea of wild animals, but most of the time you don't see any wild animals. That is why they are called wild! If there are excess species, or too many concentrated in one area, it would be very simple to round us up and take us to an area 40 or 50 miles away from a big city and let us go. Some of us will, of course, be consumed by other species. That is all right, because after all we consume other animal species ourselves. We understand this law of nature. Others might survive and form new types of animals which would become a variation of what you call wild dogs. I will not encourage you to do something to alter your animals so they cannot reproduce. Many people have the desire to act differently toward animals, but they feel unworthy and are waiting for a little nudge from the animal kingdom.

We do not dream in terms of sequential circumstances. In some stages of our sleep we will practice "dogness," as we are expected to be a particular type of creature. We will practice chasing cats and other creatures. We will be trained as to how we should express ourselves as dogs. Sometimes you will see a dog that appears to be running in his sleep, as running is something that is expected of us.

We experience time/space as a continuum. We understand the idea of distance. Earth is a place where time is a measured sequence of events. We experience time and space as a constant, as well as in sequence. This is why we are so well adapted to mankind. If you play "Go Fetch It" at the same time everyday, you can expect us to be ready to at that time (even though we don't wear watches). We live in the now and in the time sequence simultaneously.

Instinct is man's adaptive term for the emotional world. The intellectual western world does not allow for the feminine virtue of emotion. Mankind will very frequently ascribe what is emotional to what is instinctual. Mankind still needs to have a mental description for the emotions. All instinct is primarily caused by an emotional attraction.

We are primarily involved in procreation according to smell, emotion, and the attractive energy. Smell is a very strong part of our reality, as it is with many creatures. While it may be a minor function in man's world, it is much more important to us since we do not have the use of our fingers. We cannot explore objects by touch other then a gross "paw" touch. We use our abilities of taste and smell to understand whether something is to be included in our world or not. It is in our procreative state that we will often use taste and smell so that we can know if something will be a nourishing experience rather then an upsetting one.

There can be no absolute devotion without subjugation. You have created for yourself a constant reminder that you subject yourselves to the idea of control. You will respect us only if we are absolutely devoted to you. While you are willing to accept us as having personalities, you also expect us to create for ourselves a belief that you are the master and we are the servant. While we do joyfully serve you in your lessons, we also know that those daily lessons are not always recognized. Subjugation requires that we be your humble servants. In order to respond devotedly to your every whim, we will sometimes do pleasantries for you. Be aware that your whims are also your lessons.

If you do not find comfort in your life, you may create us to accentuate your discomfort. Should you have an experience with one of us that is not comfortable or uplifting, perhaps you are telling yourself that you do not yet understand ideas of discomfort in your life. There is no reason for you to have lives that are unpleasant in any way. As long as you believe that your life must be unpleasant, you will create the idea of guard dogs, or dogs that tear up your favorite picture, or dogs that mischievously create discomfort for you or your family. Dogs are in your lives to serve your lessons by responding to your needs. When your needs are those of discomfort and rooted in belief structures that you are somehow unworthy of total comfort, we along with other creatures will cooperate to show you that you do believe in some form of disharmony.

It is important for you to recognize that, as absolutely unswerving and devoted servants, we find that we must necessarily give up a portion of our true identity. Subjugation requires us to have at least one trait in common, that is that we give up our free will. Our wild members who live out in the jungles or upon the land move in groups or packs. They have a form of freedom that we do not express when we are with you. While we are willing to be absolutely devoted to you, we have also accepted the idea of being controlled by an outside force. You perceive that you are totally controlled by forces outside your ability to influence. Although we have positive joyful reasons for being in your life, we also teach the lesson of absolute devotion. As long as you believe that you are controlled from the outside and that you do not create your experienced world, you will require the cooperation of your fellow beings (and specifically us dogs). We remind you that you subjugate others. You continue to require us to be less then we are, and not to be all that we can be.

We are happy beings, we dogs. It is natural for all creatures to be happy! You can use this in your lives by knowing that it is natural for you to be happy as well. If you are feeling like you do not have what you want in this life, then know that sometimes you do not remember what you have. You set up goals for yourself that are not really appropriate for you, or you decide that you have to have something when it is not the right time. We always know that we have what we want and that we are here to serve you. We feel that we bring into your lives the happiness and joy that you sometimes will not bring in for yourself. You don't need an excuse to be happy, and you don't have to find an excuse to be sad. Just know that you are always taken care of, and you will always receive what is right for you at any given moment. You will be receiving, in that sense, what you want. Jump into the world with both feet! We jump into the world with all paws. Share in our happiness.

Man has chosen us to be his mascot because of our natural happines. It is true that some of us are trained to be watch and guard dogs, but that really goes against our grain. Most of the time when we bark at people it is a greeting. People are often startled, but those are our voices, that is the way we talk.

In the dog world, our lives are very simple. We are devoted to mankind, and since we have a daily contact,in a dependent fashion, we are more connected with what you perceive of as yourselves. We respond to your whims and your wants.

If you walk past one of us caged or tied up in a yard without much room to run around, of course we may bark. Please don't always assume that we are mad or angry. Most of the time we want to greet you and say hello. When you greet us, remember that you are much taller then we are, and we would rather greet you eye to eye. If it is comfortable for you, it is so much more pleasant for us to look straight at you, instead of having to look up. When we look up at you we perceive your anxieties more easily. Recognize that in order for us to be more friendly, you need to get closer to our level, so we will know that you do not have a need to dominate us.

Please don't immediately rush over to pet one of us when you see us. If we come over to you and nuzzle you, then you will know that we want to be touched. It would be better to look into our eyes, not stare, just look and see who you see there. We reflect back to you what you are feeling about yourself. If you see joy, then know that is a good time to touch us. If you see fear or apprehension, it is possible that we will react to your fear by barking or biting if you touch us. We react to you. We are counterparts to what you want whether you are aware of it or not. However, there is no reason to blame yourself if you have been bitten by a dog. It is important to realize that whatever you were feeling about yourself at that moment is exactly what was reflected back to you. The best thing you can do for us is to be comfortable with yourself. When you approach us or when you live with us, don't feel that you must be more powerful then we are. We are only as powerful physically as you need us to be. If you do feel that you need to dominate us, ask yourself, "What am I afraid of, and why?"

We have chosen to be with you all of the time, unlike most of the creatures who live in their own realms. Remember, if you really want to improve our lives, improve your own. Don't pity us if we seem to be struggling, rather do what you can for us by being happy and comfortable within yourself. This way we will not have the added burden of the discomfort you are feeling. This will liberate us all to be the happy, joyous creatures that we really are!

Chapter VII

Dolphins

We are the species that you refer to as dolphins. My name is Ree. Our relationship to mankind is that of offering true spiritual alignment in a physical body. Our intellects, emotions, and bodies are in alignment. The emotions we experience the most are happiness and joy! We have this happiness because our duties are primarily for the future. It is true that we act as guides for many human beings on the spiritual plane. Primarily what we will be doing will take place in the future with your race. We hold the history of mankind in our dolphin consciousness, not just what has gone on before, but what may follow (in all of it's probabilities). Our purpose on this planet with you is to guide you gently toward the understanding that intellect and happiness can be at home together in a physical body.

Intellect, as you have used it up to this point in time, has had a braking effect on the emotions (as in stepping on the brakes in a car). We have a very powerful intellect, and we are for the most part happy. It is rare to find a grumpy dolphin. It is not our nature to be unpleasant unless we are in a position of protecting our young or protecting someone that we have chosen to adopt. When sailors have fallen into the sea, we have upon occasion adopted an injured one and helped him to get to the land. We can become truly fierce protectors in order to get people to a position where they can help themselves. That is an analogy of what we are doing for mankind.

As a species, our race consciousness comes originally from one of the water planets in the galactic region of Sirius. The social engineers that came to this planet originally were from that same galactic region and many of the animals that they found on this planet were not suited to the development of human beings. Many animals were too violent to support a race which survives primarily by it's wits. Our purpose is to help you understand how you got here and what you can do with that knowledge to help your lives now.

Speaking as a representative of my race, I will tell you that we were invited to this planet by beings who lived many thousands of years ago. At that time, the Earth was at a slightly quicker dimensional vibration then it is currently. Your Bible seems to have been written two thousand years ago and yet the historical evidence is that it had been written even earlier. This is so because the

Earth was operating at a slightly different dimension. Linear history is actually fluctuating in its time zones. Time, as you measure it now, would not necessarily be the same number of seconds to a minute as it was then. There was a very highly advanced society, both technologically and spiritually, existing here at the time of our invitation. The scientists of that time predicted probable scenarios for the future, and they had an eighty percent prediction that mankind would not survive. It was necessary for them not to lose the information that had been gathered, and it was known that most of the written records that existed would be destroyed. They invited a being that could live innocently on this planet. The being needed to have a highly powered intellect and have a high degree of telepathic communion with all species universally. This being could bring mankind along slowly and work with mankind's unconscious mind, bringing back the knowledge from these ancient civilizations. We were invited to come to this planet and hold this knowledge so that mistakes made in the past would not be repeated.

Many people who were among the original soul-tree beings, (the Bible refers to 144,000) who came from original patterns of consciousness, (there were 144,000 in number) were deemed to be the most reliable and responsible. They stood around a very large tank and invited us here. The tank was not sunk into the ground, it was actually level. It was made primarily of a highly amplified version of a crystallized structure, (silicon dioxide, or quartz) and had some veins of other crystalline substances within it—rose quartz, gold, barium, and a few others. Then the tank was filled with a saline solution (which you would now call, in a variant form, sea water) and crystals that acted as attractor antennas. Much as a crystal can be used to project a ray, it can also be used to receive a ray. The ray of our consciousness was beamed in our planet's direction. It was an instantaneous communicative ray made up of all of the colors in the visible light spectrum. It would be seen as a broad visible ray, several feet across, that would look somewhat like a rainbow with a shimmering countenance to it. We were then able to broadcast the plasmic energy of our being towards this tank. We set up a sympathetic vibration within this ray to establish a frequency pulse between our planet and that of the tank. The transmission took place over a very short time. The representatives of the 144,000, maybe 30 to 35 people, stood around the tank, at equidistant placements. They held within themselves the emotions, thoughts, and spiritual inspiration that were necessary in a species that would be a repository of mankind's knowledge and accumulated achievements. They broadcasted this energy through their third eye region into the saline solution in the tank. This in turn, energized the receiving crystals to receive the ray of our plasmic energy, and we traveled into the tank.

We do not look the same on our planet as we do here. We have the ability there to be mobile on land as well as in the water. In order not to appear threatening to mankind, we choose to remain aquatic. We formed efficient bodies working with the people that were there, and were given very powerful brains. Our brain storage capacity is necessarily very large, so that scientists of the future (which is now the present), would be interested in us as a species. Many people love us simply because of the way we look and act, but there is a need for technicians to be attracted as well.

Our inter-species communication is the instantaneous telepathic transmission and reception of energy, which can be coded into thought/pictures. This is our primary reference to the idea of language. We understand all the languages of mankind. We understand the meanings of the words. The scientists that are currently trying to communicate with us might have much more success if they used some of the lost languages (such as the symbols carved into ancient ruins that have a form of aquatic reference). We do not always react to that which you ask us to do. Much of what you ask us to do will be energized with the emotion that the communicator is feeling in the moment. You must be aware that the emotion and the physical feelings in your bodies will have everything to do with how well your communication is received. The sounds that we emanate are necessary communicative tools. They can be immediate survival references or used in our lovemaking rituals.

Our procreation is primarily an act of Love/God. Our union with our soul selves is constant. We recognize that the energy of God is Love. Even your most complicated religions always come back to that. Our Love/God selves will come into union and form an embrace within a capsulated portion of the aquatic area that we are in. It is not unusual for us to engage in lovemaking while whales nearby sing the song of life. We will always turn over, belly up, as a dance in the water. A similar dance is done during the birthing experience, when the physical results of lovemaking take place. We have a ritual that is primarily created out of a need to have some relationship to your Earth birthing techniques. We give birth very much like yourselves, although it is in the aquatic environment. Our dance of Love/God is designed to embrace your world, as it is, without judgment.

A human mother that is in the water with us, or an expectant mother, may feel somewhat at a loss as to how she should behave. We are in the water because we are a very maternal species. We like to take care of the human race. Human water births give us an opportunity to actually do so. It would be so nice if your entire world would adapt to the idea of water birthing because then the aquatic species could transmit their gifts to you much more easily. Babies born with dolphin midwives would have much easier lives in the future, as the planet's water volume begins to increase. Our primary mode of contact will be looking after the young. Our initial mode is looking after the mother-to-be. When she sees how comfortable and playful we are in the water it amuses her. We can then impart pre-agreed (before physical life) information to the child, in order to bring the race of mankind into a greater state of balance. A degree of genetic code information is passed by energy to the child that will enable that child to stimulate it's own genetic memory.

While many human beings will choose to receive inspiration from us, in the form of channeling or telepathic communion, others connect with us in their dreams. Dreams are a connection to your linear lives, as well as to your potential future, past, and present. When you dream of dolphins, you most likely have been involved in the invitation of the dolphin to this planet somewhere in your soul tree. Those of you who have dolphin dreams, and quite often young children do, will later draw us as a crescent shape. Recognize that your contact in the dream state with the dolphin energy is usually to stimulate some knowledge/memory that has been implanted in you from birth (just as the ground invites the seeds to be placed within it for the crops that will blossom at a later time). Very shortly thereafter, imaginations and inspirations will come into your life that were not consciously present before.

I will remind you once again that we were created on this planet as emissaries from another plane of existence. We will remain with you throughout your experience here. We, as a species, were the first and will be the last animal here, so we will know all that happens with you, to you, from and between you. This is why we are here, to be encoded with the entirety of man's knowledge. We will gladly pass on, to those of you who will receive us, knowledge at the appropriate moment. That will be when you are emanating love toward yourselves. The best you can do is remember that we are always receiving mankind's experience. What you are feeling is very important to us. We will show you joy, love, happiness and play so that you can do this for yourself. If you are happy within yourself, that is what we will receive from you.

Do the best for yourself, even though your life may sometimes seem difficult. Allow your life to flow, just as the water flows around us. If something seems impossible to achieve, look at the path you are taking to get there. If you are creating many hurdles, perhaps you can consider another path to a similar goal. If there is a great struggle to get there, perhaps you are trying to swim upstream. Go with the flow, as you like to say. When the flow is moving in a gentle direction, we will move with the currents. Watch the currents of the sea from a ship, and you will see different colors reflected on the surface. The currents are the highways of the sea, the rivers that we will follow. You can do the same.

You can create joy within turmoil by creating love within discomfort. Do not love discomfort for it's own sake, but feel love and attract joy to yourself. When you see a movie about dolphins, pretend that you are inside our bodies and feel our ecstasy! Feel it with your body as well as with your imagination. Feel the dolphin sounds as you are jumping through the waves.

Recognize that you have chosen to re-image your world (all of the species that live on it) into what you perceive as the Garden of Eden or Heaven on Earth. You are re-energizing the alignment of your intellects with your emotions. You are bringing together the masculine and feminine energies that exist within each and everyone of you. There is a desire at the mass consciousness soul level to re-create true harmonic existence with all creatures as well as with all methods of existence. You Earth Beings are individuals, but you are also a species of mankind, you are all connected. If one portion of your body is fighting with another portion, you will experience pain and may even develop disease. Mankind fighting with mankind on Earth is a disease. You have decided on an unconscious level to do away with war by letting go of judgment and separation. As you begin to be more nurturing, understanding, and forgiving of yourselves, you will begin to take the final journey toward true harmony. Many inspirations will come to you in the near future that will encourage this growth cycle. We await your arrival into the universal community.

Chapter VIII

Elephants

We elephants, as you call us, are the land leviathans as compared to the whales which are of the sea. We represent to your species the continuity of time. Even though that which has occurred on this planet has occurred at different dimensions, there is a degree of continuance. That which has begun continues, and time exists as a circle, rather then as a straight line. Life is continuous. When we die we do not simply return to the Earth. We go on to become our energy selves for replenishment of our own energy species life force. When you look for prehistoric remains of previous civilizations, you will sometimes find complete or partial versions of us as a previous specimen race upon this planet. We have existed in some form for as long as the planet has existed. You may say that the Mastodon is a previous version of our species, but it is not really previous so much as it is a variant.

What were once the great continents of the northern and southern hemisphere are now occupied by the ice caps (northern and southern poles) of your planet. At one time, much of the surface land that existed on your planet was at these northern and southern poles. Your land masses will shift in order to accommodate the surface energy of the planet, much as you move your own body weight around according to the way that you feel. Some portions of the planet Earth are more sensitive and more vulnerable then other portions. As it has been in the past, so it may be necessary over a period of many millions of years, to move the land masses around in order to cover other portions of the Mother Earth planet as a being. During times of great storms or blizzards, you put on greater layers of clothing. Spirit Mother Earth moves land masses from one portion of herself to another portion, according to how hot or cold energies are concentrated on her body. As mankind becomes less concerned with perpetuating himself by dominating all that is around him and becomes more aware of how mankind, as a species, fits into what is around him, it will be possible to have a melt occur at the polar ice caps, raise the sea level, and allow more frequent gentle rains on the land. The Earth will therefore regenerate some of it's green plant life and reoxygenate the atmosphere. As mankind gradually becomes more self confident and does not need to control his world from the outside, he will feel peace within, and it will be possible for us all to live in greater harmony. Some of the land

and the treasures that exist under the polar ice caps will be revealed and mankind can have a greater knowledge and understanding of his own history and evolution on this planet.

I reveal this to you now, so you can understand that the presence of the ice caps and the location of the land masses, are intentional, rather then accidental. The land mass locations do encourage you to be on certain areas of the globe on a more permanent status. The ice cap locations and the harsh conditions that surround them discourage mass population in those areas. As your planet shifts its magnetic resonance and as you shift your emotional interchange with your world and each other, some of the polar ice cap will melt, and what they are covering will be revealed. Then you will have access to the inside of the planet. You will then discover the civilizations that live inside Mother Earth and discover the secret of your true origin.

There are animal species living inside the Earth as well. Many of these have been preserved within the fossil rocks you have discovered. When the polar ice cap melts and there is a raising of the water level on the Earth, the shaft entrances to the inside of the planet will be opened and those animal species which are supposedly extinct will feel free to come out upon the surface of the planet. This is not happening now because mankind is still trying to control his world externally. As mankind allows himself to be at peace with himself, as he exists, he will have less need to be externally violent as a reflection of his internal conflicts. One of the results of his internal peace shall be that species which have not felt safe on the surface of the Earth intermingling with mankind will come out. Many more animal species exist inside the Earth than exist on its surface. The variations of mankind which live inside the planet, 40 to 60 miles down inside of the Earth's crust, live at peace with these animals and recognize their guardianship with each other. No one eats anyone else, they live on growing matter.

Now you would like to know more about who we are to ourselves. We will sometimes refer to ourselves as Looma. This is the name of our home planet in the galactic region of Sirius. The social engineering race that originally came here to develop this planet seeded our species onto Earth. It was believed that we could assist mankind in discovering his own identity, as he is preparing to do now.

Our minds have been prepared to have some understanding of the unspoken human language. We do not need to understand your words since there is such a babble of them. Mankind has forgotten to use, consciously, the language of telepathy. We listen to the telepathic subconscious messages to understand what you really wish to communicate.

Mankind is gradually becoming more aware of who he is. As you allow yourself to be in better communication with yourself and with others through imagination and see who all the animals are for you, you may begin to realize that your life here on this planet is intentional. Recognize that your world is a rainbow of possibilities and that you can be all the colors, not just one.

There will be less call for us as a needed species in the future of your civilization. This is fortunate since the desire for the ivory portion of our bodies is what has really decimated us as a race. When mankind has more respect for his own body, he will have much more respect for the bodies of others.

For example, you have not really understood the devastating influence of the effect of fear on your body. When you are fearful, you seek to change your world externally. We show you yourselves. When elephants go on the rampage, it is because we are experiencing a dynamic energy that we must break out of. There is a mold that mankind has put us into and we must thrust ourselves out into the world. If we feel a threat nearby, rather than run from it, we will run toward it. The elephant is considered to be very brave as a result. When the energy of fear is strong, we may be attracted to it and feel a need to eliminate that energy from our environment. We feel the need to survive. Sometimes your race is so limited in its perceptions of how fear destroys you, that you use the creatures around you to remind you of your fear. When danger is present, we will frequently run directly at its source. The lesson for mankind is that the danger that you perceive outside of yourselves can be confronted directly and worked through.

The maternal aspect of the relationship that exists between a mother of our species and her offspring is very important. It is the mother's duty to pass on the knowledge of all previous elephant species, the knowledge of Looma, to the young. While the young come here with an awareness of who they are, it is an awareness that is at the microbiological level, rather then at the thought or feeling level. We show them how they must express themselves here. When we seek a mate, we will feel an attraction from our previous matings, in previous lives. That relates to the continuity of time. We will come to Earth through the continuity of time and mate not only for life, but for lives. With mates, we represent the soul's masculine half and feminine half.

We have dreams that take place in the wakeful state as well as in the sleep state. A dream is almost always of Looma, but is sometimes of sequential probable time futures that may occur on this planet. It is a dream of how mankind evolves in its twisting and obstacle-ridden path toward becoming what it once was at its higher dimensional version; that is, living in harmony with all existence.

Since you as a species often respect size, we are large in your eyes so you will understand that bulk is frequently a form of the creation of all knowledge. The Creator will sometimes create the large and the small. Who is greater and who is lesser? Begin to recognize that there is only equality in the eyes of the Creator. To understand who we are and to communicate with us, it is necessary to stop denying who you are and to allow yourselves to express truly what you feel as well as what you think. Be aware that you came here to experience what you have experienced so far, as well as what is waiting for you in the future. We know where you have been, we know where you are, and we know where you may go. The future is not an absolute.

Chapter IX

Hawks

I am the hawk, the representative of the animal world which most closely parallels the masculine principle. Our energy originates from a dimension of flight, as do all winged creatures. We represent the idea of flight, whether it is ascribed to thought, emotions, physicality, or spirituality. We exist in the etheric dimension of the planet that we attend. We have a name other then Hawk that we call ourselves, which would be pronounced "Khoma," and spelled Homa. It is a sound, not a word. We communicate with other species primarily though touch and through telepathic energy. We do not understand the languages of man, nor do we need to. Our domain is the sky and it is unnecessary for us to have any contact with man. If we do so, it is when we deem it appropriate, not at the bidding of man.

Some of us choose to participate in man's life, such as on display in a zoo or in a wildlife park. Others stay with certain men who encourage them to participate in the hunt. Our species was created with certain efficient methods of hunting, such as swift wings and sharp talons to get our food. We hunt the species that we find the most comforting and nourishing for us. We must use what we have in order to survive. Those of us who live in captivity need to be ourselves. If you lock us in cages, we will not complete our normal life span. We must be able to fly above the world so that we can have a more complete picture of it. Here is an analogy for mankind: if you continue to look down, you will not perceive your own wonder as a species. You must look up and across and see the big picture in order to know where you fit into it. If you do not see the big picture, you will continue to dominate all that is around, and you will not recognize that everything fits together harmoniously. Our species is usually considered a symbol for war, along with the eagle. We are seen as being a symbol of strength and vision, since we can see the overview. As mankind allows himself to be a visionary, he will see how he fits into society, rather then seeing how he can control it.

We choose to procreate our species when we feel it is a time for us to move on to the next stage of our development—to return to the etheric winged plane. Our species reproduces itself, as mankind does, to leave someone behind as they move on. Our offspring are examples or pictures of our existence. The etheric winged plane provides us with instructions as to geographical changes that are necessary in order to preserve our species. We may be warned of an impending threat from other species, usually mankind, and wake up out of a light sleep state in order to protect and preserve our own. This knowledge that supports our physical life on this planet usually comes to us in the so-called dream state.

We can experience spatial references. Time is a moment to moment experience. Space is measured in the distance between one area and another. We usually choose to live in a certain geographical location for our entire lives and will only move that location if instructed to do so through the winged plane. We will use landmarks to experience an idea of space and time through space.

As soon as mankind is willing to have a species that is equal in power to himself, our species will be more apparent in your society. Mankind now feels threatened easily. In order for us to have a better relationship with mankind and show ourselves more, mankind must undertake an emotional growth that will take 20 to 30 years. In the meantime, we may continue to shrink in number.

The epitome of what I have to offer is the projective principle, that which is strength and a creative force thrust into the world. I am not here to change when there is resistance not to force change, but rather to illustrate the principle to the world leadership. The finest is being offered. You need only to partake or drink from the cup. In this sense, I do make my offer. We soar above mankind, not to say that we are any greater then mankind, but rather to indicate that mankind can be greater in every sense then he has allowed himself to be.

Do not leave women out of this! For indeed, the masculine principle is involved in the female just as much as in the male. The creative power exists just as much in the female as it does in the male, though she frequently does not know it. Strength and courage are known in the female just as much as in the male. The female does not always say it is so. The female does not have to deny this any longer! There is no advantage in denying your strength, courage, and creative power. If you deny this to protect others, you are only denying them their right to grow out of their limited pictures or perceptions of themselves. If you act weak, silly, and uncreative and pretend you cannot do something by yourself (when you know you can), you do not promote masculine growth in males anymore than you can promote their feminine growth. For indeed, they must be allowed to grow. Women, mothers, wives, sweethearts, and career women must allow men to grow into their abilities. Just allow them to be who they are and make their own mistakes. If you pretend in order to make them feel stronger, they will stay who they are. They will be too afraid to move beyond that point. They know this, but they are not likely to admit it. Allow them to be, and allow yourselves to be.

When women are being creative and powerful, you should not sublimate this nor shove it below the surface and give the credit to others. Let yourself receive. Do allow recognition for your creative acts of wisdom and beauty. Indeed, should you allow others to take credit for your deeds, you will not serve yourself nor will you serve others, except to encourage the delay of their lessons and your own. You notice how I speak mostly to women, this is because the women have so sorely neglected their masculine sides and right now there is a crying need for you women to admit that the masculine, creative, strong, projective side has always been a part of you. You have been denying this. You have been pretending in the belief that somehow mankind will find you more desirable. You have been pretending that this side of you does not exist, that you do not have this creative power, that you do not have this strength.

You must show these characteristics now! In this way, you will allow mankind to stop being the foolish one, as he is many times. You will allow men to become the receivers, just as much as they are the projectors. In this sense, it is a valuable contribution, and it will take courage. In order to stand up for what you believe in and take credit for your deeds, you will need courage. You will many times have to go up against those who act much more powerfully, but indeed, no one is more powerful than you are right now! It is only an act. If they choose to act, you can act this way as well. This does not mean you must overpower men in a physical struggle. It means that you look them squarely in the eye and say I can do this, I have done this, and I can take credit for doing it just as well as anyone I know. Encourage others to do so, be they men or women.

Encourage people to take credit for their creative acts. This creative force and power, this masculine energy in both men and women needs to be expressed. Now is a time that calls for many brave decisions to be made in the face of physical evidence to the contrary. Decisions have to be made in a leadership capacity, to lead your country, your planet, your world beyond their old ways which do not promote the welfare of your own species, much less the welfare of ours and others. Remember that you have the power; do not deny it!

For your power can be a power for good, not just wasted energy in a self-destructive force. Use your power for your own good as well as for the good of others. Take credit; never forget what you do. If you make mistakes, do not be afraid to acknowledge them. You will grow through your mistakes just as much as through your finest accomplishments and sometimes more. Many times, taking blame for a mistake can be one of your finest accomplishments.

Look to yourself for a source of power! Seek no further than your own powerful being, your own soul, your own strength. Indeed, therein lies the solution to any and all problems. Do not seek beyond yourself. For you are your own strength, and power, and reserve of energy. In this way, you will serve yourself and develop your own masculine energy and bring it into balance with your feminine energy. You will serve yourself in the finest and most balanced way.

Chapter X

Horses

We of the horse empire, (and we do think of ourselves in this way) are in your lives to represent your desire to create layers of mankind (social strata structures). Your class structure in society began many years ago, when different civilizations occupied a version of this planet which functioned at a slightly quicker dimension. The idea of a class of people who would function as workers was developed. It was innocently done, with the idea that the workers would be happy with their jobs because it was programmed into them. This civilization did have the ability to alter genetic structures and to create synthetic life. However, when the creation of life occurs, the Creator is always behind it. You can bring molecules and cells and atoms together, but if the Creator is not in agreement, nothing happens. The worker class was created to serve those who studied and played and those who considered themselves above menial labor.

Those of us who work very hard and serve others are referred to as the draft horses and will do the work of heavy machinery. The draft type horses that you have created a fondness for also exhibit beauty and strength. We pull your favorite beer wagons, as well as your plows. We turn over the soil which grows the crops that nurture all of us. We are in your lives to help you understand how you have structured yourselves and have created levels and layers of society.

The race horses enjoy running. Yet only when they reach that great moment of victory are they surrounded with attention. For all horses that complete the race there is the same joy. There is a joy in athletics, the joy of participation, rather then in winning. Winning creates a structure of winner and loser; it denotes separation.

We have the royal horses, those which are princely in nature and very fussy in personality. They will associate with just a few people. That is how you have created us. The Arabians would be a good example of royalty.

The entire horse empire has unique mating rituals for the procreation of our race. Radiation of different body temperatures is emanated during mating time. We will radiate different frequencies of heat that will be felt by the appropriate member. When received, that individual will be drawn toward us to begin procreation.

We have the ability to radiate heat, so as long as it is not bitter cold, and we can maintain comfort within ourselves and our surroundings. We always prefer to be in open spaces and will seek our own shelter in the wild. If we are in large enough numbers we can generate heat for the entire group. All ranch owners recognize that horses need to have open spaces to move around in.

Horses have many different personalities, from sensitive ponies to strong powerful horses. You create for yourselves the need to be separated and to feel that one person may be better than another on the basis of how he looks, rather than who he is. It is who you are to yourselves that creates total universal love. All horses know that they are connected to the greater horse entity. We refer to ourselves as an empire because structure and strata create that idea of rulers and those who are ruled.

If you wish to purchase a horse, use eye contact to help you make your selection. Some of you may feel an attracting energy. If you do not feel any pull, then make eye contact. If there is whimsy and humor there and we stimulate good feelings in you, then we could be in your lives. Horses pull you along, you ride us and we pull your farm implements. We pull you emotionally to athletic events of competition. When we are attracting you, notice that we are at ease with each other. If we run and play, we are at peace. You can run and play as well. Just because you may have grey hair does not mean that play is behind you.

For those of you who have horses, the best way to communicate with us is not necessarily through touch. If you do touch us we prefer stroking below the neck and around the chest for communication. While making eye contact with us, pretend that you are having a conversation. Just for fun, ask us to whisk our tail. If we do respond, you may be able to explore deeper communication with us. Your communication can be more from the heart. Be aware of the emotions that you feel when you choose to be in our presence. If you are frightened or exercising authority, we may not respond to you as an equal. We must react to you as an equal in order for you to ride us. If you are willing to allow new forms of communications to develop between us that involve touching, with more feelings of love, harmony, calm, and peace, we will get along much better. There will be less need for you to force us to do something; instead you may obtain our direct cooperation.

We understand human emotions better than we understand human languages. All emotions are colored by what you feel. Many times, when you have a question for us or wish to interact, the communication does not seem direct. You may think that you communicate primarily through what you say, but it is only partially that, it is mostly what you are feeling. Individuals who approach us with genuine feeling of what they would like from us or what they would like to give to us will have a much more direct communion with us. It has almost nothing to do with what you say, but almost everything to do with what you feel.

Communication is done through heat, telepathic emotions, and touch. Telepathy does not function as a direct communication from one language to another. The individual who wants something from another or wants to communicate with another will feel their communicative methods. The other individual will pick that up through their communicative methods. If I were to feel something, you might sense a picture, but I am not necessarily sending that picture. I am recollecting the feelings that I had when I was doing that thing, and you might receive a picture of me doing it.

Horses did not originate here but were seeded here by the social engineering race that altered the life of Earth through its cyclic growth rate by experimenting with life forms. This occurred at a time when primitive forerunners of the animal species existed. Some species were not deemed compatible with the future of mankind and were eliminated. Other species were perceived to be more appropriate for the shape of mankind's bodies, such as horses. The body of man is easily adapted to riding us. Our bodies are very strong indeed, and we can allow someone to sit on our spine and can carry them around for hours at a time.

It is important to have a greater sense of communication and to exert less discipline or domination while riding a horse. Just because you ride on our backs does not mean that you have control over us. It simply means that we have allowed you to come with us. You may say, "We steer you here and there by pulling on your reins." You come with us since you are on us, but it is a cooperative effort. You ride us but you do not drive us as with a vehicle. It is important for you to have greater communion with us, with a softer touch. Treat us as though we were loved ones, rather then the worker class to be herded to the work site and beaten until we achieve our task.

We enjoy being ridden bareback, though we will allow saddles to be placed upon us, if the person riding us is frightened or apprehensive. We will genuinely enjoy being ridden by someone who is in harmony with themselves and their environment. Your energy will then fit into our envelope of energy, as we normally feel it. If you come into our auric field and are bringing your discomfort with you, you will need to use a saddle to insulate us from your direct contact. Those of you who ride on saddles and use reins will notice that it is not really necessary for you to touch us. This is for our protection as well as your own. You will know how harmonious you are with yourself if we allow you to sit on us bareback and be close to us. When you ride upon us, it is very much as though you are hugging us with your legs. You can hug with legs as well as with arms.

We are aware of our time to pass over when we begin to feel tired and when we feel less inclined to have contact with mankind and more inclined to have contact with our own species. There are times when we will feel less inclined to be with those mates (our horse friends that we have developed over the years). We will know when our time is drawing to a close. We will begin to have more dream time, and this time will have images of young versions of ourselves frisking about. This is a vision of our future rebirth into horse form again. It is also a recollection of a time when we were more filled with the wonder of life. When these images begin to appear in our dream time, we will know that it is time to move on.

We do not dream in the same manner as mankind. When we are in our standing meditative state, you will often notice that we are very still and staring into space. When we are doing this, we are connected with the horse consciousness as it has existed throughout all the beginnings and ends of societies. Our dream state is a time of fulfillment. Without our dreams, we would be unable to continue here on Earth as it is. Our dreams connect us with the positive energy of the horse empire, which exists in your galactic regions.

In order for you to communicate with all animal species with a greater degree of direct communication and a lesser degree of demand, it will be necessary for you to get in touch with your emotional bodies. It is not sufficient to be frightened and touch us in the hope that we will eventually feel better around you. We will sense your fear. An animal will react with fear, if that is what you are feeling. Emotions, as you feel them within yourself, have everything to do with how you communicate.

Your communications with each other will be greatly improved if you are willing to be aware of your emotional status during verbal intercourse. When you say something to another person, you may not feel that they understood what you said. It is because they understood primarily what you feel and cannot deny that feeling. Emotions that are in the physical body are heard louder than verbal words. If you can begin to communicate with feeling to us, you will gain a much greater understanding of your own potential as a race and will not feel the need to control all that is around you.

Recognize that communication on its full level is the key to avoiding the necessity of functioning from fear to control your environment. When there is greater communication among all classes of mankind, or races, or cultures, or nationalities, then it will be less necessary for you to create strata or layers of society in which some people have all the luxuries and some people do all the work. Communication on a heart-felt, emotional level will head off the need of groups to control and dominate others in order to feel safe and secure within themselves. When human beings try to create softness and security inside their own immediate auric fields by controlling their external world through command, control, and domination of their own kind, they will not be communicating directly. They will not be communicating within themselves nor with other races or nationalities of mankind. They will be attempting to control others through the exertion of their will or their mental tools. It is necessary for mankind to begin developing a greater sense of emotional communication and to radiate that emotion as they speak. Mankind's communication will have everything to do with the coming together of all races and nationalities in the future.

Communication through the inspiration of the spirit, by the direct tool of the emotion you are feeling while you are speaking is the tool of the future. Some cultures are more dramatic in their speech then others. This excitement is useful. Communication is how you move your body, as a form of dance, as well as what you say. It is necessary to improve the quality of communication so that you can have greater safety among yourselves.

Chapter XI

Insects

You may ask, why do insects fly toward the light and seem to beat their wings so strongly? Would you not be treating us with kindness if you turned the light off so we would not exhaust ourselves in this way? I will say to you, just allow us to do our dance with the light. Do not feel that you are somehow creating a false light, or false Sun. You are, in fact, doing your part in your own universal harmony to provide us with the image and creation of light. We dance to the light. It is our joy to dance to the light. Be willing to watch our creative, harmonious dancing. Even if we seem to destroy ourselves, it is in ecstasy of the light. The light is the one true light that creates us all, of which we are One. Light is the purpose behind the existence of all. The light is the physical bridge to the nonphysical idea of God/Goddess/All That Is. It is, in that sense, the union of all dimensions. Light is God. We are all light. We are united in light. Our dance is a tribute to light.

Do not feel sorry for us. Do not feel that we are destroying ourselves because you have turned on a switch. It is not so. We dance and fly in joy. We beat our wings to the harmony and the love we feel for the light. As you seem to create the light with the flip of a switch, know that you have consciously created a tool. You have created a thought or a machine that produces an illumination from the One Greater Light to remind you that you, in fact, create the light. You are of the light. Our approach to the light, though it may seem to be in disorientation, is not that at all. It is a dance of joy!

Allow us to remind you that the joyous dance, in tune with the light, is that which mankind must remember. You can observe our dance and be uplifted into the light yourself. When you see the light in the form of the Sun, be with joy. It is God/Goddess/All That Is that reminds you of itself. The Sun is in fact the physical identification in your world of All That Is. When you see the Sun come up in the morning, or even when you turn on a light, allow it to illuminate your life. Allow it to remind you that Sun or light is that portion of you which existed before your physical self, and will exist after your physical self. Do not deny that it is also that portion of you that exists while you are in your physical self.

Be willing to dance with us with your emotions of joy. We will then be happy that our lesson and reminder to you has been understood. In our own small way, we have provided you with a true guide to your own illumination.

It is up to you to understand that we are all a portion of the One. We are here to remind you that no matter how mighty or large you may be in physical comparison to us, we, in our own small way, are just as important. We are just as much an idea of God as you are. There are times when you will feel that your world is closing in on you and you have no way of being in happy experiences. Many times we will show ourselves to you to let you know that it is possible to live in the simplest way and to exist on the simplest foods.

Even in this simple way, we show you our harmony and our existence as an idea of God. The illumination we have spoken about is reflected in our lesson to you. As we cooperate with this lesson, we cooperate with your soul's desire to remind you that you are God, that your life need not be complicated, and that you can live in harmony with all living things by respecting and honoring yourself. Allow yourself to live in simple harmony, trust, and faith. Understand that God will always provide you with what you need in the most positive ways. This is the trust and faith that we have. We joyfully remind you of this by showing you our lives and the way we live. We do not suggest that you live like us, that you become like us. Remind yourself that the insects placed before you by God to remind you of simple existence and unquestioning faith and devotion. They have chosen not to complicate their existence. You as man can do the same. You need not provide yourselves with great complications in your lives.

Many times you will purchase or obtain objects that delight you for the moment, and yet, in time, these objects become complications. You sometimes become slaves to your objects, rather than allowing them to be a simple joy in your life. Be willing to allow your life to be simplified. Be willing to allow these objects to be joys in your life. Do not believe in any way that you are somehow plagued by your objects.

Remember that in harmony we live and love together. Respect us if you would, for we are in fact an idea of God/Goddess/All That Is. Be willing to respect our need to live. Be willing to come outside of your dwellings and speak to us where we live. If we are inside your dwellings, speak to us there, out loud or in your thoughts. Speak to us with honor and respect and ask us if we would be willing to live outside of your dwelling space. Be willing to share your foods with us, for at times we do require it. Sometimes man will pave over the surface of the ground which denies us access to that surface. It is at times like this that we will emerge in your structures to remind you that we are creations that need to exist in love and harmony with physical sustenance for food.

Feel free to talk to us where we are. Be aware that, as you speak to one of us, you speak to all of us. Insects are united in consciousness. What one of us knows, we all know. We all believe in the one universal light consciousness and are aware of what the universal insect consciousness knows. Be willing to state to us that you will bring a portion of your food wealth to an outside location where you would prefer us to be. Be willing to allow this location to be in a safe place, not in the street or on the sidewalk of your city. Make it some location where we will not be disturbed by man's machines. Be willing to place your food offering with respect. Thank us for our willingness to cooperate with your lessons. Be willing to do this for three days of your time. Three is a number associated with mankind on your planet. It is also a number which we are comfortable with.

We love and respect you. Do not believe that we are here to cause you discomfort. We are not here to inflict pain upon you. We do not wish to cause you discomfort, but if you, through a negative need, create a desire through your fears that we shall do this, then we must do so. Remember, if you are bitten by one of us, it is in response to one of your fears. At that moment ask yourself, why have I created this discomfort? Why have I created this reality for myself? When you do this form of questioning within yourself and listen for a still small voice to answer, you will create an understanding of your lessons. You will remind yourself that you can cooperate with all forms of consciousness.

Be aware of the needs and fears that you are creating. Be willing to release your fears. Do not bind your fears to you, or you will create experiences which seem to justify them. Remember that if you believe your life is a reflection of the light, then your experience will be of the light. Be willing to allow yourself the joy and harmony of the light!

Chapter XII

Lions

From the jungle of man's consciousness springs forth a giant beast. This giant beast of your consciousness is but a seemingly ferocious version of your own unexpressed desires. As you learn to express your desires and understand the true nature of power, it will be less necessary for you to be surrounded with gigantic, potentially dangerous beasts. We are only potentially dangerous because of your own potential. We react, as do all animals, to mankind. That is the purpose of our existence in your world. All forms of human beings react to each other, and so we react to your whims, desires, and beliefs.

You feel a need to create danger around you and a need to have control. Before feeling a need for control, one must necessarily perceive danger or that which needs to be controlled. This is why you have created creatures such as us, creatures that you believe need to be controlled. From the wildness of your own desires and minds, comes this idea of a wild beast. The word beast means "that which cannot be controlled by any other means than with force." This only suggests, that you believe your wild unexpressed thoughts cannot be controlled by any other means than force.

This is why you have created the idea of "Will." You "Will" our own wild thoughts and beliefs into submission. When there is something in your minds that is not peaceful or comfortable for you, you "Will" these thoughts into submission. You force them below the surface and this creates turmoil and discomfort for the total you. Therefore, you create a need to illustrate these wild thoughts and control and manipulate your environment. The illustration of your environment will match your inner thoughts. As you create the need to control your environment, that which is all around you, you create a need or belief in the necessity of that which must be controlled. Your will is really a form of unexpressed passion. Passion is that colorful element of physical consciousness which you have been suppressing all these years. You have recreated the idea of passion into "Will." When you are not receptive to the inclusion in your life of comfort, beauty, joy, and satisfaction in every way (in the most positive natural way), you will create a need to express these ideas to yourself in any way you are willing to receive them.

You create the beautiful creatures and (as you perceive it) the wild beasts such as lions and tigers. Your beliefs in these monsters (as you create them) will then cause you to confront the idea of discomfort. As you approach us with your discomfort, we feel it; we snarl at you, and we yell at you in our loudest voices. We will growl and snarl to accentuate your discomfort and show you just how uncomfortable you really are. You do not recognize a true mirror image! Remember always that when you look at creatures, including lions and tigers, we always reflect back that which you are experiencing at that precise moment. If you experience joy, love, and harmony, even if we are in personally uncomfortable situations, you will receive that joy and harmony back from us.

You will always be known; that is, we will always know who you are by those thoughts and feelings that emanate from you. We react to these feelings to let you know how you are feeling, since we are your agents. We are agents of understanding for you. Remember that when you confront lions, we are showing you who you are at that moment. Not who you can be, not who you will be, not who you were, not the potential beauty that you carry with you at every moment, but who you are in that very moment that you approach us. You may use our services in the most comfortable and compatible way for you, so that we may be served also. Since we are creations of your need, do you not feel it would be a good thing for us to be of beauty and joy and harmony with you, as well as in our own environment?

It is not necessary for us to be wild and uncontrollable. It is only your wild thoughts and uncontrollable (as you see them) feelings, that cause us to reflect this. Always remember that who you are at the moment you are with us is who you are seeing, hearing, and feeling from us.

You perhaps wonder why animals, including lions, eat each other? We react to your beliefs. You wish to create the beast, therefore, all the animals you see as lesser life forms respond to your creation of beast or monster. We eat each other and you say, that is survival of the fittest. It is a way you have chosen to live.

You have created a need within you to create evidence of that which you believe. You are physical beings, so naturally, you create physical evidence to respond to your beliefs. We eat each other however, for other reasons as well, not only for sustenance (since that is how you have created us) but also to show you that nothing is lost. When a creature comes into me, when I am joined with that creature by eating him, I am not less. I am more. That creature within me, that creature which has been eaten, is not less. That creature has become a portion of me. In this way, we show you how we are all a portion of the One Being. You perceive yourselves as individuals. We are here to remind you, even through your direction of our violent ways, that nothing is lost and no one is greater than another. We are all One, becoming One, ever changing physically and still remaining as One.

The question has been asked, "In ancient times is it true that lions pulled people around in carts?" This is true for some beings. There were classes of beings in ancient Egyptian times, and other civilizations before that, who did not feel that we had to be wild beasts. Rather, they understood the idea of beastliness as being a projection of mankind. Man is not a beast, but as man suppresses his passions, so man will create a need to express that beastliness or violence that your passions become when they are not expressed as love or creativity.

Therefore, the people of the time recognized that, in order to understand who they were and to know that they were in complete harmony with the One, they would expose themselves to us. They would not command us, but they would help us maintain our bodies by providing us with what we needed. They also provided love, which they understood to be power. They would use us almost as you use a weather vane. When that weather vane turns in a certain way it shows that stormy weather is coming, it is time to take shelter. You also know that when the weather vane points in other directions it is time to be comfortable and reflect beauty as you go out among your fellows. They knew that if we reacted to them positively, peacefully, and joyously and were willing to pull them about in carts, they were in harmony. If we reacted in the beast form, they knew that they were projecting unexpressed and suppressed ideas of love.

If you are in complete harmony with yourself, all creatures will react in complete harmony with you. If you suppress your passions, exerting your will in an uncomfortable way for you and others, we will then reflect savageness.

In the future of your lives, do not feel that you cannot use our bodies, because we know that we are never ending. We exist as we become a portion of your bodies.

You have also desired a smaller version of us, since you hold us to be magnificent beasts. You wanted to have a smaller counterpart of us that you could domesticate and have around you at all times. So, you created cats. Cats are an outgrowth of the idea that you are beginning to be more willing to receive affection from us, the large lions. Cats represent a smaller and less frightening idea of who we are. You will notice that cats will bring creatures into their mouths and will consume them. If they are not hungry, they will (as you perceive it) kill these creatures and not eat them. What they are doing is bringing the souls of those creatures inside themselves and taking a portion (however small) of those creatures into their Beingness. They do this in order to become joined with the Whole, in all ways.

If man did not exist, there would be no creatures. You create us out of your needs. If you were all in harmony, creatures would not need to eat each other to show you that you are out of balance and focus and are not receptive to your true loving selves. Kittens or cats are that portion of your passions that you are willing to deal with. As you lavish love upon these creatures, remember as well to give this love to other human beings and to yourselves.

Creatures do not, of their own right, get sick. You have some portion of experience, something in your life, that has not been expressed in the most loving way. Therefore, if you have allowed any creature in to your life, it will show you the discomfort that you are projecting. If you are not willing to receive it in a positive way, they may become ill. Always recognize that when those creatures that choose to live with you express any discomfort within themselves, they are only manifesting some discomfort that you have shown. As you cage up lions, so you cage up your own true desires and your own loving needs. Uncage your own loving expressions and, in so doing, release all of the creatures who show you what you do not give to yourself.

Chapter XIII

Monkeys

With infinite understanding, I realize that it is apparent to you that monkeys stand for play. We also stand for the wisdom of knowing that play (in its happiest form) is the balm of the disease of adulthood. As children grow older, they may get caught up in a feeling of too little, or too much, self importance. They are programmed by their environment to have a certain idea of who they are and what role they must play. It is only during times of spontaneous play that this role is allowed to be less rigid, less domineering an influence in their lives.

The species monkey, in all of its formats, (with the exception of the larger species called Apes) knows that to be healed with the Earth and with ourselves we must be childlike. Even though you might see great wisdom in our eyes from time to time, we recognize that being the child is the most useful way of healing transgressions (imagined or real) against us.

We originated from an area of the universe referred to as Arcadia, which is a planet in the system of the crab nebula. It is a tropical planet, made up of what you may refer to as rain forests as well as lakes and rivers. It is more of a fresh water environment then of saline water.

The theory of evolution is very narrow in its scope of understanding the development of man in relationship to the monkey. Just because an animal has some physical similarity to man does not validate a theory. This missing link theory has no real basis in fact. We are a species unto our own and do not have the need to evolve. Evolution as a thought or a practice is not invalid. Evolution occurs in a species on the emotional, intellectual, and spiritual planes. The resulting changes affect the outward physical appearance of that species.

Sometimes, one of your species will "get religion" or be converted to some great idea, and it might actually change the countenance of their person. Perhaps they had looked worried or sad prior to some new understanding that uplifted them and afforded them ease in their lives. Perhaps the lines, wrinkles, and dark shadows under their eyes went away, and they became more cheerful and accepting of their role in life. Perhaps they actually allowed themselves to be somewhat playful in their new identity. This happens very frequently. The evolution of mankind is gradually moving toward allowing more spiritual and feminine virtues into the actual daily life reality. This will somewhat soften mankind's external features. As your species evolves you will have some outward changes. However, we have no intention of evolving toward your species.

Very often a species which is unsure of itself and cannot trace its direct lineage or ancestry, as human beings cannot, will develop theories of evolution. It provides a sense of security to have the knowledge of where you came from. The desire to create this theory is brought about because mankind does not remember where he is from. As mankind allows himself to have a greater stimulation from the spirit inspiration, and the emotions as a communication tool, mankind will allow the feminine virtue of instinct and sensing to know where he is from, in terms of planets and galaxies.

We understand variations of the human language, and we can be taught a rudimentary vocal or auditory method of understanding your words. We do not need to understand what you say, because we communicate directly with emotional energy—telepathic energetic communion. We are willing to indulge you and learn some of your specific words and symbols and the meanings that you attach to them. We don't need to understand your language to know what's on your mind. Researchers who are trying to reproduce results from one of us to another, should be aware that, like you, we are individuals. We have less of a herd consciousness and are also unique. While one of us may be willing to go along with your tests, perhaps another will not.

We do recognize that, since it is believed by mankind that they have domination over all creatures on the Earth, they must be allowed to feel safe on this planet. Eventually, mankind will realize that he rules himself only. Mankind exerts an external control over his world because mankind does not feel safe inside his own body. A child who does not know who its parents are will feel much less safe then a child who does. Having roots and identity, can be very helpful. Mankind as a whole unit is so disconnected from other versions of mankind on this planet and elsewhere that he does not really have the gift that we have. We understand that mankind's need for domination is an externalized need to feel control over his environment. Mankind actually has communion with all species, but as yet is not aware of it. Mankind does not yet have the understanding that communion means tolerance.

We have emotions and love and will very often mate for life. The big difference between our mating and procreation rituals and yours is that we will not feel the need to control one another. One mate or the other in a pair will allow the other to do whatever naturally happens in the mating dance. We feel safe in the knowledge of who we are. We will be drawn together by love and will stay together for the same reason. There is a joy in the passing on of who we are to our offspring and encouraging them to be the finest examples they can be.

We dream in the same context as man does, though our dreams are more of a recollection in energy then in thought patterns. We experience time and space in terms of distance. We operate on the Sun/Moon clock, lightness and darkness. We will have a degree of Moon cycle in which we will be more receptive. The male of our species is equally affected by the Moon cycle as is the female. We go out during the day and project ourselves into the world, and at night we sleep and allow our physical bodies to rest while we experience some of the feminine virtues of emotional love.

The death experience is a community affair. If one of us should die violently, there is mourning from the immediate family and a sense of loss to the community. On the other hand, if we should have a natural slow death, there is a gathering of the family as well as the community to receive the energy and the knowledge that the dying being has received in his lifetime in the form of telepathic communion, as well as in the form of touching.

Less of our communication is done through vocal sounds. The sounds very often express immediate survival needs or emotion-related communication. The passing on by natural causes of a member of our species allows us to share with the community the lessons learned in that physical life, as well as to communicate what is being seen in the visions of that member as they move into the spirit realm that connects us to Arcadia. We will then describe gradually some of what is happening as we begin to re-envision our home planet as we move into spirit.

As you observe us in your zoos or in your movies, recognize that the reason we allow ourselves to play is that the healing aspects of childhood spontaneity are so useful in the adult life they can be a tool which prevents aging and disease. If you allow yourself to be more emotional, you will have less diseases. Your emotions need to be expressed just as do your mental thoughts. Your physical bodies need to express themselves physically through touch. Begin to allow all aspects of yourself to be experienced, rather then trying to structure everything through your mind. When a child plays, it is not necessarily thinking deep thoughts. Allow yourself to have more play time in your life and you will have much less discomfort.

Chapter XIV

Owls

I am the spirit of the Snowy Owl, which brings with it the winds of change. I am often misunderstood. There has always been, associated with our presence, changes that occur. This has brought about a mystique associated with us, along with superstition and blame where none are warranted. Change can be many things. Often it is due to something that has been hanging on, which when released, can be liberated and the next step taken.

We are to some extent the keepers of the doorway between dimensions. This is between the third dimensional plane that Earth people and animals live on and the stage of life that is transitional or sometimes referred to as the astral plane. We live in both. As a result, people may see us when a loved one is ready to pass on. Our energy helps them to do so with speed and ease. You can see how this has caused some misunderstanding about who we are. People have sometimes assumed that we are a sign of death. We are actually a sign of change. Those who understand us know that when we are seen, it is time to make a decision, to choose a new path and to move towards it without delay.

We exist for you as a form of living spirit guide. We are, of course, mysterious and different. That which lives both within the spirit world and your Earth world will have elements of both. When we exist in our spirit world or astral plane we assist human beings to fly past the astral and on towards the light, that is to say, towards God. We can go in and out of the astral plane at will. This is unusual, and we are the only energy that can do this except for those teachers at higher planes who can access all life identities easily.

Some souls which exist in the astral plane are there temporarily, others are there for longer periods of time. We enrich your world by helping the souls of mankind to find their way home. Sometimes, home is the next dimension, or the afterlife. Sometimes, home is a move from one place to another, or from one stage of life to another. Remember this when you see us.

As the spirit of the Snowy Owl, I am somewhat of an unusual sight. Whenever one of us is apparent in your life it means that change is present for you. It does not have to mean dramatic change, do not misunderstand me. Sometimes when you see us at a distance, flying, it might simply mean that you are in a time of change for yourself or for your world. If we circle over you, fly close to

you, or sit near you, then you will know that the change is more personal and perhaps more imminent. This is important to remember so that you don't misjudge us or hold us responsible for the changes which you, in your spirit self, ask us to remind you of with our presence.

We are from the Earth, and we do not come from anyplace else. We are one of the original spirit species here. Most animals will either come from some other origin, (according to my understanding) or from another planet or time. We, like some of the native tribes that began here, came to be with mankind as a guide. The tribes needed to have certain foods and shelter, which were provided for by Mother Earth. Equally, their spirits needed to be fed. We are so closely associated with the Earth spirit of mankind that as soon as humans appeared in their present form on this planet, we appeared simultaneously. We exist on some other planets that have similar lifestyles, especially those associated with the native tribes. People who live on the land and off the land in a communal manner will often need to have spirit animals associated with their journeys.

Sometimes the medicine man or woman of a tribe will pray to or ask the spirit owl to come and assist in a hunt. We are considered a vision of good fortune in times of famine. It is believed that simply by our presence and our abilities, we will enhance a tribe's opportunity for food gathering.

We also assist in the soul's journeys during dreams. We are known as a spirit animal that assists the spirit out of the body permanently, from life to afterlife, or temporarily from the stage of sleep that is involved with deep dreaming. Our dreams are not always associated with the work that we do. We will often dream of the world as it exists in it's natural state, without any disruption from mankind's follies, as we see them. We will dream of the pristine or virgin Earth and see ourselves interacting with all species. This beautiful version of Earth is like heaven for us.

Since we have a universal calling, a message, something that we do specifically, when one of us passes over into the spirit realm and moves beyond the astral, there will need to be another owl seed or soul spawned on this planet. Planet Earth provides the owl existence wherever it might be needed. This planet is like a birth chamber, and if an owl dies anywhere, it will need to be recycled as a soul through the spirit Mother Earth energy. Then a rebirth can take place.

There are no great ceremonies; instead there is an implied acknowledgement of the passage of life. We have a broader definition of what it is to live. We understand the cycles of life and acknowledge the death of one of our species with an awareness that very shortly the soul will recycle itself, re-embodied as an owl. It will then place itself in some convenient location. This will be close enough to assist people in their soul journeys and far enough away so that we can conduct our own Earth lives.

We may have an instinct, calling, or knowledge that there needs to be more of our species present at any particular time. This is not just because some owls have died somewhere, but rather so that the number of live owls remain consistent with our ability to handle soul travel. One owl may be able to handle 100—1500 souls, but not much more then that. This is why when there are great disasters, and many Earth people or souls are transiting, some will spend longer or shorter amounts of time in the astral plane. This is in accordance with how many spirit owls are available.

We will procreate on the basis of need as well as of the recycling of life. If there is a feeling or knowing that we will be needed, we will procreate frequently. If you suddenly see an abundance of us in a particular area do not become frightened and think that there will be a great disaster in that area. Do realize that the area is destined to change. It may be a very good change, positive and enjoyable, but nonetheless it may mean that many people in that area will be moving away. Perhaps they will move to another dimension, but it is equally possible that they will move to another location.

Owls are not driven by emotion. We understand our jobs and the necessity to live physical life here as it is part of the soul's journey. We do not have the range of emotions that a human being might have. Our strongest emotion, from which we are absolutely unswerving in allegiance to, is the emotion of "duty." We experience time only as day or night. We relate to space and time together, according to the demands of our duties. Some of our duties are spiritually oriented, and others are Earth oriented (for example eating and raising our young).

We understand that the animals we kill for food are here for us as a part of the Earth cycle. There is an implied consent in all animal species who manifest here that they are a portion of the recycled energy, even mankind has become that at various times. Mankind is usually offended by being part of the food chain. The animal species, including myself, have no such offense. We are very clear that in order to remain here on this planet and live in this dimension, we must kill to eat. While you, as humans may remove yourself from the killing cycle, when you go to the supermarket to buy ground beef or chicken chunks, you are essentially asking someone else to do your killing for you. We must do so directly. When you have others do your killing for you, you will remove yourself, a little bit, from the cycle of life on Earth. Those people who hunt and do so with respect for the species appreciate what they receive, use all of the animal, and use all that has been given by spirit Mother Earth in her bounty, are more likely to understand and appreciate life cycles. It helps to make one clear, when you are closely connected to what you do to survive.

We do not understand the human language in words, although we can sometimes understand the deep desires of a being. We do not communicate as you communicate, nor do we need to understand your motivations. We are in touch with the soul level of a human being and the unconscious mind which has a universal language. If a person wants to get a message to us, the best way is to meditate on us, or to use guided imagery, or simply look at pictures of us and imagine yourself in our bodies, flying, and being with us. We do not have a great deal of elaborate external communication inter-species. There is some, but it is minimal. Primarily, we communicate through the soul level. The sound that you often hear us make, "who-who," is pleasant for us and has aspects that we use to range or orient ourselves spatially and locate other members of our own species. It is to us like a form of radar.

It is important for mankind to understand that since this world is in a tumultuous period of change, the owl as a spirit guide as well as a living being, will be more important to help you in transiting through changes. Remember that mankind is a portion of the life cycle on this planet and is not the dominant species or the ruler here. We do not perceive you as a greater species. It is our duty to assist you, as a species, to understand how you physically fit into the cycle of life on this planet, so that you may perceive yourself as equals. You are not greater than or less than other life forms. When you begin to accept that you are equals, you will be ready to meet civilizations from other worlds and fulfill your desire to exchange knowledge and experience with other cultures.

Since we have so much to offer, I will simply say that the more of us that are living and available, the easier it will be for you to dream and to have golden voyages in your dreams. Sometimes, when you dream of flying and you have no perception of your body, it is because you are in our bodies, flying. When you assume that we are something to be removed to make way for some structure that you feel is necessary, remember that we are equals. We all have a role to play in the universal link of life.

Chapter XV

Sea Turtles

We are the species that you have come to know as the sea turtles. We carry within us the wisdom of all the universe. It is not exactly an easy task that we perform, since there are other planets where discomfort is experienced as it is here on Earth.

The wisdom of the universe must be protected. This is why there is the symbolic protection of a shell around our body. You have a desire to protect your innermost secrets within your own psyches and to store your important things inside safes. We have a symbolic body structure to protect us and give us a place to hide. Our symbolism for you, then, is that which exists into eternity. There has always been a variation of our species on your planet as it exists now, and there always will be. You may or may not see evidence of that from time to time. There will always be a species version of us, for we are symbolically the repository for knowledge, of the wisdom of the universe. This knowledge is not only that which is known to you, it also means that which is unknown to you, and that which is as yet unimaginable by you. This is why many races over the years have chosen to consider us an unusual species. We are a particularly inspiring species.

I speak to you as a sea turtle because we have a much greater opportunity to be undisturbed by mankind than our brothers and sisters that live upon the land. The purpose of our species is to act as a link between you and the unknown in your mind. This is information that you will need to recognize in order to live in harmony on this planet. That includes a better understanding of where you have come from as a species, where many of our fellow creatures have come from, and your potentials for the future.

The best lesson for you to learn from us is to be flexible in your patterns of behavior. As we glide through the water and move from place to place, although we are of great bulk, we can be flexible in our method of transport. We will sometimes leave our shells behind, in order to swim the great oceans or to move with greater speed from point to point. This we must do in great trust of our own persevering energy, for sometimes we will be consumed by other species. We can do this because of our trust that we will live on without our bodies. We come to you now to encourage you to understand how you live on, be it in body or spirit.

Our calling is one that involves wisdom from all of the universe as well as wisdom from your own known species. We have originated from all points known and unknown and exist in a form on all points in your greater universe. We have originated from the energy of creation. When we die and leave our physical bodies, we simply return in creative force to the energy that we have derived from the Great One, the inspiration to us all.

We can live for as long as 1500 to 2000 years in a single body. Your technological scientists have not yet found one of us in that age bracket, although some of your scientific technicians have suspected as much. When a body is created that is comfortable and durable to all information in the universe, it must be a very efficient and powerful body. Because we have included so much of what is known and that which is unknown, without any sense of distrust or judgment, we have no resistances to physical life. There is no psychic, physical, or emotional resistance in our living selves. We do not put any strain upon our living bodies during an entire lifetime.

We choose to procreate through the Great Creator of All, who stimulates us to let us know that our species is becoming less of an influential force in numbers on your planet. This is why many of our species on land will have so many young. Our numbers need be at a certain level in order to function as a repository for mankind's future understanding. When we are encouraged to come together, it is because our number is unbalanced compared to the number of human beings on the Earth. We will produce, within one group, a single individual that has the potential to live an extra long life, as well as those that will live 500 to 750 years. We have one or two individuals that can live great periods of time, not because experience proves a valuable teacher, but rather that, when our numbers dwindle (which happens from time to time), we will then need certain giant members of our species that will carry the load.

We communicate telepathically through the All Knowing Oneness, and we make a form of ultrasonic sound that is almost beyond the range of mankind's ability to measure at this time. We communicate through telepathic understanding. We understand all spoken, thought, and projection languages on this planet and elsewhere.

We have a form of sleep that is a deep meditation which allows our physical selves a degree of relaxation not possible during our waking states. We also experience a time of a connection with the One All Great Creator when we recall the origin of our species as a need for mankind.

I would encourage you to understand that our purpose here is not to be like you, but simply to acknowledge your presence and to give to you a greater understanding of your world. Your scientists, as well as children, express wonder and curiosity. I encourage you to wonder and to follow up on your explorations.

In the future, please do not hunt us so ferociously. Understand that we realize that our consumption by other species prolongs and strengthens those species in racial terms. However, I will request that you do not use us for purposes other than consumption. Do not, if you would, use us as a product for application to the skin, or as a product in a catalytic reaction between chemicals. Our numbers are not so great that we can become a source of chemical reactive agents. Our source souls do not encourage great numbers of us to survive. Very often, many young are born because it is necessary to strengthen other species to exist within the charged atmosphere of this planet. When I say charged atmosphere, I mean the energy of discomfort, equal to the energy of comfort. You sometimes say positivity and negativity. Thereby, it is important to allow other species who must survive, in order for mankind to see its potentials, to consume our bodies. They must have the will and the physical durability to survive. Interspecies, please allow the balance of nature to take place and please do not abuse your privilege of consumption.

These days, your species is coming into a greater knowledge and understanding of itself. It will be necessary for us to be called upon, almost as a computer bank, to supply you with the answers and the wisdom of the ages. Please respect our role as we respect yours.

The catalyst that mankind seeks to eat the pollution that you yourself have thrown into the sea (I am not referring to that which is naturally created) is not going to be found in the near future. It is necessary for you to begin to recycle that which you waste. Some species of humankind do that now in the growth of food products. It is necessary for those of you who live in the cities to recognize that, even though you may not be involved in the direct production of the foods that you eat, a total recycling of matter must begin (whether it be waste or creation of new products). You must learn to utilize the heat that is a result of waste processing.

Mankind must begin to see himself as a portion of nature. Mankind has been given free will, so that he could have the experience of creating harmony from a position of disharmony. This encourages mankind to be curious and to explore possibilities. If you have a feeling of disharmony in your own physical selves, as well as in your societies, you have the opportunity to explore through your intellect a way of creating harmony. Study nature in its most natural form, so that you may begin to replenish and recycle all that is a portion of your creation. Nothing in the sea, in its natural environment, is wasted. As you begin to waste less, you will begin to want less.

Chapter XVI

Snakes

I am the representative of the snake world. We are the kings of the reptilian empire. Even though we are small and not the largest of the reptiles, we perceive of ourselves as the kings because we were the first of the reptilian species to exist successfully on this planet, transplanted from our home planet of Sirius. We feel our current presence here on Earth is to remind you of your roots.

This planet Earth was colonized by the Sirian Alliance many years ago when the time of the development of the human being was in progress. We have actually been here since that time and have seen your entire progress, and are in some ways the keeper of the knowledge of how you came to be here. Other species, such as the dolphins, are encoded with mankind's entire history. We have that, and we also have the history of those who helped to create you as well.

The original plan for this planet's development was to create a place where souls could manifest themselves in bodies, such as your own and have an opportunity for an adventurous life in which they could bring out the very best in themselves, physically, mentally, emotionally, and spiritually. Earth is a chance to have a game room, where competition is possible. We are here to remind you that struggle and hardship can challenge you to bring out the best in yourself.

Notice how our appearance is used in the healing arts, such as the physician's symbol. (The image of two snakes winding around a center rod). Our appearance may also be seen on military arm patches to suggest strength, courage, or ingenuity.

Very often cultures, such as the Egyptians, who have developed a strong sense of spiritual expression will involve us in their rites as in their ceremonial headdress and hieroglyphic symbols. It is directly understood that the knowledge we possess, which connects both the past and the future, is designed to be passed on to mankind in the present.

We are in fact symbols of mystery. We were designed to be different to spur your curiosity to understand who we are. Our very presence will sometimes excite your imagination. We seem to find our race consciousness in our snake empire, being a stimulant to individuals, regardless of their positive or negative situation in the moment. For example, people involved in nightmares may be stimulated even deeper into their fears. This is a responsibility we in the snake empire have had to live with. It is perhaps understandable that we are considered by certain religious sects to be signs of evil. Some of your scholars feel that it was the snakes influence that corrupted the garden of Eden, and tend to identify us with the idea of Lucifer. To some extent, as far as we can understand, this has to do with our connection to Sirius. Perhaps mankind has an unconscious race memory of resentment towards the original Sirian Alliance.

We dream of the life back on Sirius, and of the afterlife. We do not feel totally balanced in our physical bodies on this planet. Our lives are not our own, as we are serving the cause of human development. We dream of our balanced snake empire in which we can create our bodies to look differently. In other worlds, off this planet, we can be larger or smaller, and have arms and legs if we choose. We can even be involved in a form of existence that is almost humanoid. We find this life to be most pleasant. It has music and art, as well as aspects of adventure. It has combat and conflict that bring out the best in us. We enjoy games similar to the martial arts competition in which, ideally, people are not injured and they experience combat without losses. We dream of these glory days.

We have a form of telepathic communication inter-species. We also produce a form of extremely high range, ultrasonic sound that we use to warn other members of our species of danger. It is a whistling noise we make through the bones in our heads. I am not referring to hissing sounds which are part of our overt defense system. I am referring to a sound that is beyond the range of normal human hearing ability.

We do not understand the human language, as you speak in words, but we have a form of telepathic knowing. As exists in the case of some other species we will feel/hear the loudest, most predominant or influential energy in your physical make up. If you are frightened when you see us, we will react in fright by defense or attack, whichever is most appropriate for us in the moment. If, on the other hand, you are interested or happy, amused or relaxed, we will tend to be direct mirrors of whatever you are feeling the strongest in the moment. If you have more then one feeling, we will react to the most predominant feeling.

It is my understanding that in what you refer to as the martial arts, the energy of the fighters is supposed to remain in a very specific balance. This is in order to maintain the inspiration to win the battle correctly. Therefore, if you are calm and relaxed in the presence of other animals, they will tend to be that way as well. If they sense fear in you, some animals will attack. Snakes will only attack as a matter of last resort, to defend themselves or their family.

Our experience of day and night, light and dark is simply as separations of time. We do not experience time as you do, by segmenting the day. We are often born, raised, and die in a small area. When one of our species dies, its soul energy will return to the star group of Sirius and be recycled as a snake somewhere else or possibly brought back into the genetic pool of energy to be recycled in some other reptilian format. We do not appreciate the shortening of our lives by the use of our skins as shoes or adornments in any way, shape, or form. We realize that we are here to serve mankind, but we feel this skinning is done to show authority over us. We understand being eaten, as we will eat other members of the animal kingdom to survive. Simply to be hunted down and killed, or raised so that our skins can be taken, we feel is a misuse of our species. I am aware that some other animal species do not feel this way. They are perhaps more domesticated. I cannot encourage this practice.

Mankind is caught up in the illusion of physical appearance. You not only judge animal species, but also each other strictly on the basis of appearance. One of our main jobs here is to appear to be vicious. We do consider ourselves to be warriors in a sense, warriors in the pursuit of truth and freedom. We are of the knowledge that mankind's prejudgment on the basis of looks, has kept us apart. It is this prejudgment that will hold back the true communication. We will continue to procreate, as long as it takes, until mankind is ready, willing, and able to hear what we have to say, in the way it is provided. It will largely come from telepathic communion. There have always been those people who were capable of speaking to us, but because there has been so much suspicion and superstition attached to us as a race, these human beings were not often listened to.

I ask that mankind begin to appreciate their own appearance in all of its divergence. If mankind can appreciate the beauty of his own species, he will then begin to gradually understand that those that look different from himself are no less equal than themselves. In time, there will be an acceptance for all animal species. Often cockroaches and spiders as well, are looked upon with disgust, even though they have great gifts to offer you in understanding who you are. Remember that sometimes good things come in small packages and sometimes different packages as well. Be prepared to receive knowledge from sources that you may not find pleasant to look at. Sometimes, the most striking and useful knowledge will come from those who do not have great physical beauty. How many of your artists, musicians, and scientists have been plain or ordinary looking? Nevertheless, the gifts and contributions they have left you are magnificent!

Mankind must come to peace with us as a species and the way we look. We feel that our appearance, our method of defending ourselves, and our foreignness from the human being and the rest of the animal kingdom, have contributed to this sense of isolation that we feel. We feel somewhat alienated and would greatly appreciate more curiosity on the part of mankind and less blame for deeds in which we are not directly responsible. We are maintaining our culture and are waiting to be approached by the right people in your species who will want to communicate with us and ask us the question, "Who are you?" If mankind never asks us who we are, (though we hope quite sincerely that they will ask and will be ready to accept communication with us in time), we will wait until we can return physically back to our home planet.

Chapter XVII

Whales

We are the whales, and we represent the song of life. This is why we make the tones that we do. Our purpose in life is to help you understand the harmonic balance between you and all of life. We are large, yes, and for the most part we are very peaceful. We represent to you that power can be reflected in harmony. We are not known, even by those who hunt us, as dangerous, but rather as leviathans (which means something very large indeed). This is our representation to you, in your life, and it is why we make the tones that we make to each other.

We bring to you a message of harmony and understanding. We will some-times, as you have noticed, strand ourselves on your populated beaches, so that you may see how disharmonious your own lives are in accordance with your surroundings. It is not because we have become lost or sick, even though we may demonstrate physical symptoms.

This planet Earth has been made up as a planet of whole beings. You are whole beings unto yourselves, as the planet is a complete being unto herself. You have not really begun to perceive that a cat or a dog, a tree or a piece of grass, a mountain or an ocean, or other people, are actually portions of yourself. You have tried to force your belief systems onto others of your own kind, as you have tried to force your domination of will on us as a species. It is important for you to understand that, just as your physical body does not expect your hand to be a foot, when you try to force us to be strictly a portion of the food chain, you are not recognizing that we represent *you*.

We originated from the galactic system of Sirius which practices social engi-neering for the greater good of all. There are many water planets in that region. Some species of mankind, or humanoid forms as you might judge them, can be formed and adapted to fit different environments so they can go where they are needed. On Sirius, we do not look the same as we look on this planet. Instead of the smaller flippers that we have here, we have very large ones in the front and rear of our body. Instead of using undulated power to get through the water, we use more a form of propulsion. This creates more of a dance for us and a more pleasant harmony. Some of your design engineers have pictured us with these outgrowths, these flippers, because it seems as though our bodies would naturally have them. We have been adapted to this world through social engineering. This was done in order to have the undulating motion, which represents the harmonic wave action known as a sine wave. Wherever water planets exist, or planets that are largely water, we may choose to experience life there. Sea water is actually a form of the saline solution which runs through the bodies of all mammals on this planet. Sea water is very harmonious to life and very receptive of aquatic life in all forms. We feel very at home in that environment. The fluid has an ability to conduct sonic waves, and it also receives magnetic pulse energy which we use to communicate with our home planet and with the species consciousness which exists around the Earth. The sea water acts as an amplifying antenna to assist in sending telepathic messages.

We understand the words of your language, and we understand the words of the forgotten languages, as well as the synthesized languages which will be used in the future of mankind. Your current romance languages will gradually adapt to a more homogeneous language. Mankind will do this in preparation for the use of telepathy, which is the universal language. Since our mission here is to represent harmony in motion, as well as in sound (the song of life), it is necessary for us to perceive where you are living in harmony in your lives as human species and where you are not. Very often your language does not represent what you truly wish to communicate. Most of what you truly communicate is in your harmonic or auric field. That energy communication between human beings, although you may not be consciously aware of it, is not always in harmony with the spoken word.

We as a species do dream, although our dream life is not disconnected from our waking life. The more we are in the sine motion, the wave form motion in our body, the more we are in the harmony that can be conducted by us on this planet. It is at this time especially that we will have our dreams. Our dreams are a direct connection between our individual species and the greater whale species. Our dreams are waking dreams. When our body rests and floats in the water, what you would call sleep, we must remain somewhat awake due to predator species such as yourself.

Time for us is more of a continuum rather than a moment to moment experience. Our lives are very harmonious, and we do not measure time by distance or space. We choose, as a species, to travel on the harmonic energy of the Earth. The harmonic energy of the Earth is a sine wave, and we travel along that wave wherever it takes us. We use the power of attraction, and allow ourselves to be gently drawn toward a goal or an objective. We do not have to experience time as you do.

When we know that it is time to procreate our species and allow another one of us to enter this world through the female of our species, we will find a way to experience the emotion of the word you call creation. We experience the art of creation as an energy field. The couple that comes together to create the new young life will not necessarily be together at the time of this creative activity. Perhaps one, or the other, will know that it is time by the attraction power of the sine wave of the Earth. The antenna sea water will pass the message and draw the partners toward each other with the exact harmonic frequency. When it comes time to procreate, we emit very specific tonal harmonics that can be measured by your underwater speakers.

We do not refer to ourselves as whales, although we are not uncomfortable with that word. We refer to ourselves as Ceta. That is the name of our home planet in the Sirius galactic region. The word Cetaceans is derived from the original word harmonic Ceta. Words and the creations of words in all of your languages is one of the ways that you allow yourselves to create intellectually. Every year you create new words and new categories of words to describe new occupations and the like. These words are always instigated in your minds, not just by the objects that they are describing, but through the inspiration mechanism that allows you to feel the act of creation. When we die our physical bodies decompose and are utilized by others such as yourselves. Our spirits return, very much as yours do, to our species consciousness which surrounds the Earth. At that time, our species consciousness will decide whether we as individuals will recreate ourselves through others of our species or return to our home planet. It is not unusual for Ceta to return to their home planet in order to experience their identity in its pure harmonic state and to be refreshed.

In the treatment of us as a species, it is important that you know that we allow ourselves to be captured so that we may become part of your food chain. We consume creatures in the sea to survive, and as part of your food chain, we help you to increase your understanding of harmony. This is why some of the races of people in the far east or extreme north who consume us, will have religious or philosophical aspects in their societies which allow them to be much more alert to harmony.

Be aware that the consumption and use of our bodies is something that must be done more sparingly. It is important to use the portions of our bodies as more of a spice in your foods, rather then making a meal out of us at one sitting. We are not against the consumption of us as food. Telepathic messages between our species and yours are not possible on the mass scale because you still believe, in your western world especially, in proof. Since you are not involved in the universal language of telepathy and since you do not understand us fully, you must consume us. There are less of us on your planet right now because you have abused this privilege. It is not as though we are raised like cattle that are willing to be bred in large herds. I will ask you to be more selective on your hunts and try not to take one of our species that has young ones. This is very important, because the young ones still need to learn who they are on this world. They have an understanding of species consciousness that they are born with, but they do not have a solidly established communication within this world. If you do hunt us down, notice when we are swimming solo rather then in large groups. If we are in large groups, try to perceive (and this is not difficult) when one or two adults are protecting a smaller one, and please leave those alone. Please take one or two of the herd that seem to be by themselves. They are by themselves because they are ready to be taken by your species, and they do not have a mate at that time. We would prefer if you would take these as the catch of the day, so to speak.

When we are captured and put in a sea park aquarium, it is difficult for us and very often we will not survive. We do not do well when we are deprived of physical contact with members of our own species. If you should decide that this is something that you are going to do, and I understand that this will cost you a large portion of currency, I will ask you to build as big a holding tank as you possibly can so that it can contain at least two of us. It must be of the exact same species. Sometimes you may put dolphins in the water with us; that will work only if those dolphins are in pairs. When you look in your mirror you have a direct reflection of who you are. When we look at each other we have a direct reflection of who we are.

We are in your life as a spice, and in the future you will learn much more easily how to communicate with us. The fact that you are reading this book and that many of you already use us as a symbol for joy, love, harmony, and peace is because you are preparing to communicate with us on a more direct level of telepathic communion. We are with you in motion.

Chapter XVIII

Closing Remedies

For those of you who feel that the fish, animals and creatures of this planet should not be eaten and that they are only here to be appreciated for their beauty alone, I thank you. That is not the only reason they are here, however. The creatures are here to provide you with beauty and with many lessons. We are here to nurture you in body as well as in soul, in mind as well as in feeling. Remember always that when you consume a creature, that creature always knows that it is not destroyed. Nothing is ever destroyed. There is only the absolute infinite One existence you call God/Goddess/All That Is, The Light, and we are all interconnected within that Light. No animal is ever destroyed. You need not feel guilty about eating animals. In time, mankind will choose to cease eating creatures, although that time is not yet here. Do not feel that you must artificially abstain from eating animals if your body craves to be one with a creature. The animals show this to you by eating each other. Animals are here to guide you to all that you can be, towards your greatest potential.

Ree, the dolphin

Appendix

A Few Words on Channeling

What is channeling, and what is it's purpose? One of the purposes of channeling is to help integrate our Spirit or Light Selves into our day-to-day Selves. Channeling can give you guidance and direction. It exists as a resource of wisdom that can be called on at any time. The ability to communicate with your own Soul and to feel that communication in energy (as well as to hear it in the form of words) is a truly wonderful experience.

Channeling is the accessing of greater knowledge through any individual. It is as though the individual is at the bottom of a funnel. The funnel then expands into wider and wider creative supplies or greater knowledge. Individuals perceive themselves to be something that stands alone. In your world you identify things, people, and ideas, by specific labels regardless of your culture. It seems to be comforting to identify the greater knowledge and ascribe a name to it. I am referring to God, Goddess, All That Is, The One, whatever you choose to call it. This greater knowledge has no entity in a singular fashion. The greater knowledge is made up of all energy. You may perceive your life as an individual consequence, the greater knowledge perceives itself as All. There is no individuality. The name will give you a sense of cor-poreal identity. This is how you relate to the world and how the current society relates to you.

However, in the mass total knowledge, The All That Exists, is your entire world, as well as you personally. The name given to any entity is merely to help you locate yourself within your world. Any and all channeling that is done today is a form of the greater knowledge screened through all that the particular individual is. Just as water flowing down a river toward the ocean picks up little rocks on the way, so the All That Is (the water ever-flowing) picks up bits and pieces of the identity of its immediate surroundings and defines itself by what it is flowing through. The source of the water is not what it flows through. The source is from the greater "Is." Specific identities of channeled Beings are given for your benefit, to help you feel more secure in who you are in the moment. Therefore, any channeled Being that goes by one particular name can and does come through many different individuals.

The practical application of channeling is accessing knowledge about which you do not have any conscious recollection. Your conscious mind allows you to orient yourself to your world from an individualistic point of view. The subconscious mind allows you to communicate directly with your emotions. The unconscious, or your Soul, or uniqueness of God, Goddess, All That Is, can be the portion of you that you access during channeling.

When you allow yourself to be free of control from your mental processes and allow yourself to speak without thinking, you are allowing yourself to express who you are beyond who you consciously perceive yourself to be. If you allow yourself to physically move during the channeling, then you can access even deeper levels of yourself. Psychology does this through the use of analysis to some extent. Hypnosis also tends to remove controlling factors and enlarge your safety zone.

Channeling acts as a gateway to allow you to open the inner gates to a greater you. You may access greater knowledge reflected through yourself and allow your unique gifts to color that knowledge. That which tends to interest you will be that which you channel. Those individuals that are drawn to you to hear your channeling will be most interested in those topics as well. You and your audience will meet on a common ground, to access knowledge. This can bring a more secure feeling (within your conscious mental perception of who you are) into your world.

The purpose of channeling is not to incorporate outer world wisdom into your inner Self, but rather to incorporate your own inner wisdom into your daily life. You will perceive your daily life as that which exists outside of and beyond your skin. You will perceive yourself as living within an encapsulated system and interacting with other systems. Understand that the purpose of channeling is to help you perceive your life as one entire system. It is not to bring worlds together from a position of separateness. It is to help you perceive separateness as illusion. Channeling persists in your life, since your conscious mind has expanded beyond your intuitive sense to give you a link to wholeness.